Shards from the Bards:
a Bardstown Writers' Collection

For more information about the Bardstown Writers visit:

http://www.bardstownwriters.btck.co.uk

Shards from the Bards: a Bardstown Writers' Collection

Bardstown Writers

Bardstown Press

First published in 2014 by Bardstown Press

Copyright © Bardstown Press 2014
Individual contributors © the contributors, 2014

The right of the Bardstown Writers to be
identified as the authors of this work has been
asserted by them in accordance with the
Copyright, Designs and Patents Act 1988

*All characters and events in these pieces, other than those
clearly in the public domain, are fictitious and any
resemblance to real persons, living or dead is purely
coincidental.*

ISBN 978-0-9930096-0-0

Cover design by Charlie Reaper
Bardstown Writers' logo designed by Elliott Parkes

Shards from the Bards: a Bardstown Writers' Collection

CONTENTS

Like Mist	1
The Key Cutters	3
Geoffrey's House	15
Open Book	25
Jealousy	37
The Tripod	39
Au Revoir Quebec	47
Dorothy at Mill Stream Cottage	49
Mary's Shop	59
Rejection	63
Circling Hat	65
A Toad, a Brick and a Wren	75
The Tramp on the Bench	81
Smallman & Bigge	87
Marie Corelli:	
Champion of Stratford-upon-Avon	97
Something Old, Something New	109
Essential Oils	113
The Broken Float	121
The Birth of the Bard or	
Having Babies in Tudor England	131
The Skeleton in the Cupboard	141
About the Authors	151
Acknowledgements	159

Like Mist

like mist
there is a stillness
that descends
before I fall asleep.
like mist
there is a blanket
wrapped around me,
and my dreams, you keep.
like a bubble
that glistens and whirls
in the air
you are my world
and we share
all that we are,
all we will be.
now, all those days
have tick
tick
ticked
away
and suddenly we are old.

one day the mist
will be gone
the air will clear
and one of us will be alone.
I cannot think
of that
for I love you
too much.

© Jacci Gooding, 2014

Shards from the Bards

The Key Cutters

'Not bad for a new boy!' George teased Toby after rugby practice.

'Shut it Daniels,' Toby replied to the round tank of a figure that was George Daniels.
George increased his pace and overtook Toby. He had spotted the ice-cream van at the school gates.

Toby hated his new school and was glad that it was Friday. Eager to get away from George he ran off in the opposite direction taking the short cut home through the village allotments. He hadn't got far when *wham* he was stopped in his tracks.

'Hey ginger,' Ben Bradley sneered, as he tightened the headlock. 'Give us yer money, freckle face!'

Toby's eyes watered under Ben's stinky armpit. Why did he have to move to this stupid village anyway and why didn't he have any mates to help him? Toby wriggled his head and managed to look up from Ben's grasp. Was that really George he could see charging at them, screaming like a mad baboon?

George lunged at Ben. Ben flew backwards

into a pile of fresh manure. Billy Bradley quickly pulled his brother out and, to Toby's relief, the twins ran off.

Toby had fallen into a bed of cabbages. 'I hate living here,' he moaned.

Standing up, he checked his pocket. Yes, his pet spider was OK. He was tucked up safe in the matchbox. No harm done to his only friend.

George helped to pick up the contents of Toby's school bag from among the vegetables.

'The Bradley twins live at the pub. They're always causing trouble,' George told Toby handing him a large silver keyring with a key attached.

Toby turned the keyring over in his hands. 'It's not mine. What do you think those funny words mean?'

'Casa Lignarii,' George read slowly. 'Dunno. Wonder what it opens?'

'What you two up to?' George and Toby looked behind them. A scrawny boy was pushing his glasses up his nose with one hand and holding a smartphone in the other.

'Hi Pali,' George said. 'This is Toby.'

George elbowed Toby in the ribs. 'Show him. His Dad's a policeman. He might help us.'

'We found it,' Toby explained, dangling the key.

'If it's been reported missing you'll have to hand it in. I'll ask my Dad about it.'

Shards from the Bards

Toby slipped the key into his trouser pocket, next to his matchbox for safe keeping.

'Let's meet here tomorrow morning at ten,' George said as they left the allotments to go home.

'Ok. Oh and George...' Toby said.

'What?'

'Thanks for your help back there, but I had it under control.'

'Of course you did mate,' George laughed. 'See you tomorrow.'

The next morning, Toby was frantic with worry. His school trousers had mysteriously vanished from his bedroom floor. Pulling on his clothes, he raced downstairs and burst into the kitchen.

'Where're my school trousers?' he blurted.

Toby's mum looked up from the newspaper she was reading.

'They're in the washing machine. I don't know how you get them so dirty.'

Toby frantically pulled at the washing machine door. It was locked. Water swooshed inside. He slunk to the floor and put his head in his hands. He'd lost the key and drowned his only friend.

'Here,' Toby's mum said. She was shaking her head but smiling as she handed Toby the matchbox and the keyring.

Toby breathed a sigh of relief and put them in

his jeans pocket.

'Thanks Mum,' shouted Toby as he raced out of the back door before his mum could question him.

The allotments were busy. George and Pali were waiting by the old shed. George was eating and Pali was researching on his smartphone.

George looked up from his crisp packet. 'You're late,' he said.

'And you're ugly,' Toby replied, helping himself to a handful of crisps.

Pali looked up. 'Dad said the key hasn't been reported missing. We can keep it.'

Toby took the key out of his pocket and they huddled together to take a closer look at the strange words engraved on the keyring.

'What's going on?'

The boys cringed. It was a girl's voice.

Olivia had been riding her horse in the field next to the allotments. She now stood looking over the fence.

'Nothing,' Toby said, quickly stuffing the key back into his pocket.

'Hi Liv,' said George. 'How's Misty?'

'Her name is Irish Mist, George!'

Olivia took off her hat. Her long blonde hair fell over her shoulders. She glared at the boys.

'Show her,' George sighed. 'It's the only way to

get rid of her.'

Toby, resisting the huge temptation to give Olivia the matchbox, handed her the key.

'We're trying to find out what it opens.'

Olivia inspected the keyring. 'I've seen this writing before. I could help.'

'Nah, no girls,' George told her.

'Well, maybe...' Toby shrugged.

'Excellent,' Olivia beamed. 'Meet me at my house in an hour.'

She threw the key back to Toby and strode off.

'What? Who put her in charge?' Toby asked.

'You did!' George replied, grinning.

The Manor House had high grey walls and Toby thought that it looked like a castle. Olivia was waiting by the gates. She had changed and was wearing a peach outfit with a matching headband. George thought she looked silly.

'About time too,' she wagged her finger at them. 'Come on. Let's find Badger Fred. He'll know about the key.'

Toby could see how Fred had got his nickname. His black bushy eyebrows formed a 'V' shape on his wrinkled forehead and when he took off his flat cap a mop of white hair was exposed. Fred turned the keyring over in his dirty hands.

'Not sure. Although...'

Olivia's eyes bulged. She stepped closer to Fred, elbowing George out of the way.

'Do tell Fred!'

Fred handed the key back to Toby. 'The writing's familiar. Try asking Charlie Sykes. He'll be at the pub having breakfast. Now get off with yer, I'm busy!'

Badger Fred watched as Olivia and her friends raced through the gardens and disappeared out of sight. 'It'll end in tears,' he muttered to himself as he returned to his work.

Charlie Sykes was indeed at the pub. Toby sat down beside him and handed him the key.

'Do you know what this opens?'

'I dunno,' Charlie replied, wiping ketchup from his lips.

'Oh. What bad luck,' Olivia sulked.

Toby snatched the key back from Charlie. 'I'm going to the toilet. I'll meet you outside.'

George was starting to drool over Charlie's sandwich. 'It must be time for lunch. I'm starving.'

Pali looked up from his smartphone. 'George, it's only half past ten. Hey! What's that on the wall?' Something had caught his eye.

Olivia took a closer look and traced her finger over the hanging picture. 'It looks like a map that leads to a cabin. Look! The cabin's called Casa Lignarii!'

Shards from the Bards

Pali took a photo.

'Come on!' Olivia pushed George away from Charlie's food. 'I think we've found the key to that cabin!'

Concern etched across Charlie's wrinkled face. 'Don't get too excited. That cabin burnt down years ago,' he told them as they ran out of the pub.

'Oh, almost forgot Toby,' George said, running back to the toilets.

He found Toby with his head under the hand-dryer.

'What happened to you?' he asked. Water dripped down Toby's face.

'Bradleys. I tried to run but...'

The door burst open and in spilled Pali and Olivia.

'Er, boys only!' George shouted.

Olivia took no notice. 'Who stuck your head down the toilet?' she giggled.

Toby's bottom lip starting to quiver. 'It's not funny.'

'Never mind that. We've found a map that leads to a cabin in the woods,' Pali said. 'We think the key might belong to the cabin.'

Olivia tugged at Toby's damp sweatshirt. 'Let's go!'

'Seriously, who did put her in charge?' Toby grumbled.

After squelching through woods they stopped to rest by a crashing waterfall. George gobbled chocolates, Pali was busy on his smartphone and Toby studied the keyring.

Olivia leaned over Toby and grabbed a chocolate from George. George smacked her hand hard. Toby quickly stuffed the key into his pocket and tried to stop a fight from breaking out. Olivia stuck her tongue out at George and popped the chocolate into her mouth.

'Found it,' Pali announced proudly. 'The words are Latin. They mean 'The Wood Cutter's Cabin'.

Olivia stood up and straightened her now dirty peach outfit. 'Come on then. Let's see if we can find this cabin.'

George's face was as red as a tomato as they trudged across more muddy fields. He was convinced they were lost. 'I'm so hungry,' he grumbled. 'I can't go on. Leave me here to die.'

'According to the map, we're nearly there,' Pali reassured him.

He was right.

'Look!' Olivia was pointing across the field. 'It's the cabin.'

The cabin was covered in brambles. The windows were smashed and half of the roof was missing. George carefully picked aside the spiky weeds to reveal a door.

He reached behind him with his hand held out. 'Toby, give me the key.'

Toby reached into his front pocket and took out the matchbox. He tried his other pocket and clutched frantically at the loose material. The keyring wasn't there. He'd lost the key!

George was not pleased. He used words that Toby didn't know. Olivia gave George her best disapproving look and Pali shook his head in disgust. George mumbled an apology.

Toby desperately dug his fingers around in the empty pockets. Then he remembered! He'd put the keyring in his back pocket when he was trying to stop a fight between Olivia and George.

'Here it is.'

Toby handed the key to George, who thrust it into the lock. Using all of his strength he tried to turn it. Nothing happened. 'It doesn't fit,' George announced.

'Let Pali try,' Olivia suggested.

George stepped aside. 'But Pali's a weak geek,' he laughed, handing over the key.

Pali patiently twiddled the key to the left and then to the right. 'Click'. The key turned and the heavy door swung open. He turned to George, smiling. 'Not bad for a weak geek eh.'

They stepped inside.

'Oh dear.' Olivia sighed.

Spiders scurried across the dusty floor and thick cobwebs laced the walls. George swiped at them with the chubby hands, revealing a picture underneath. 'Hey, look at this. It's the map!'

'I think we've found the Wood Cutter's Cabin,' Toby smiled. 'It hasn't burnt down. It could be our secret den.'

Olivia wrinkled up her nose in disgust. 'Are you mad? This place needs burning down!'

'All it needs is a bit of paint,' Toby said, scanning the gloomy room.

Pali agreed. 'I'll get a key cut for everyone,' he said. 'So we can come here whenever we want to.'

'A den needs a name... Oh, I know. How about Pink Palace?' Olivia suggested. 'We could have pink cushions and pink...'

'No way,' George interrupted crossly. 'Rugby Ranch is better. We could use tackle-bags for seats.'

'How about...The Key Cutter's Cabin?' Pali offered. 'And we could call ourselves The Key Cutters.'

Everyone thought it was a fabulous idea.

'Let's get home before it gets dark. We can meet here tomorrow morning at ten,' Olivia said, pushing Pali and George out of the door.

'Toby stay away from the Bradley twins,'

George warned. 'We don't want them to find our secret den.'

'OK. I'll just be a minute,' Toby told them as he released his pet spider from the matchbox. 'Welcome to your new home Sid. You'll make lots of friends here and I'll visit you every day.'

And so, locking the door carefully behind them, The Key Cutters made their way back home.

'I love living here!' Toby announced to his new friends.

© Sharon Hopwood, 2014

Geoffrey's House

Cycling to work past Holy Trinity Church, Geoffrey gave his usual nod of respect towards Shakespeare's tomb, before slowing as the timber framed building came into view. He liked to think of it as his house, even though he only worked there. Standing for centuries, the structure always evoked a comforting sense of permanence in Geoffrey.

Half an hour later Geoffrey glanced around the parlour with satisfaction. The long oak table's polished sheen reflected the burnished copper vase holding flowers he had just picked from the garden. The room shone with a warm, lived-in feel, one the guests would appreciate.

Geoffrey started as Esther Hemming's strident voice bit into the very timbers.

'Come this way. Do try to keep up.'

She had beaten him to the first visitors, yet again. He liked to be there to greet them personally, welcome them.

He stepped into the hallway to see Esther at the head of a group of affluent looking tourists. As she clip-clopped in her ridiculous shoes down the flagged passage, Esther ran an elegant forefinger along an oak bureau.

'Been dusting again, Geoffrey? Well done, keep up the good work,' she nodded in his direction as if he were a mere caretaker, instead of a Blue Badge Guide, before leading the tourists up the wide stairway. 'The family rooms are upstairs. Please keep together.'

Geoffrey was angry and speechless as they trooped past him. He would have enthralled them for hours with his intriguing tales of the house, Shakespeare and his kin. Although they never stayed for more than half an hour, but rushed back to their coach, happy to tell relations and friends they had 'done' Shakespeare.

Geoffrey listened as the hated voice became muffled, filtering down through the cracks in the old boards that groaned under the heavy footsteps. They looked like a group who would tip generously and he knew Esther would give a gracious smile as she held out her hand at the end of the tour. He cursed himself for taking too much time in preparing, but he did like to make sure this old Shakespearian property was presented at its best, pretending he was the owner and not just a guide.

After the tourists had all gone home, there in

the soft stillness, he liked to believe he heard whispers of its many ghosts. He would run his hand over the weathered, studded door, the banister or fireplace, and imagine all those who had touched it before him, including maybe even Shakespeare himself.

To calm down, he took a deep breath, breathing in the scent of polish and flowers before brushing away a speck of dust that had settled on the picture of Queen Elizabeth the first. Then he straightened his tie, brushed his hands through his sparse hair and moved towards the front door to be in position to greet the next visitors.

Unfortunately, a party of noisy, disinterested schoolchildren greeted him. They pushed and shoved each other and tried to nick sweets from the gift shop while Geoffrey sought to control them. With Esther and her group coming towards him, he racked his brains for something to hold the children's attention. Children today only seemed interested in vampires, werewolves or ghosts. An idea took hold. He would invent a resident ghost, one who had met a violent end and who still haunted the house. Suddenly, they were still, listening to his every word.

'Now, if you are very quiet, I may even show you exactly where this gruesome murder took place.'

By the time Esther drew level, Geoffrey had the children wide-eyed with wonder and clinging to each other. She gave a brief, superior nod of her head and passed by.

'Are we gonna see it then. Where he did her in?'

Geoffrey smiled at the towheaded boy and beckoned them to follow while trying to work out the details of the supposed murder. He liked the idea his ghost might be a housekeeper, a bossy and interfering woman, someone like Esther and decided the scene of her demise should be in one of the top bedrooms.

Leading the group up the narrow back stairs, the ones the servants would have used, he regaled them with how the spectre of the housekeeper may still be seen walking up and down these very stairs. The children loved it and shivered with delicious fear.

'How did he do it then? Was there lots of blood and stuff?'

Here was a boy who played too many of those nasty video games, Geoffrey thought, but weighing it up he decided there had better be some gore.

While describing a scene equal to any of the Jack the Ripper murders, Geoffrey began to experience a sense of excitement, imagining Esther lying on the bed, half naked and cut open, with all her self-righteous dignity gone, lost like her blood spilling out onto the patchwork counterpane.

Geoffrey felt a tug on his sleeve and looked down at the boy.

'I said – did he keep any bits of her, like that bloke in London?'

'Well, I can't give you an answer young man. But I can show you the very knife used to kill her.'

This seemed to satisfy the group and Geoffrey led the way to where, safely locked in a glass case, lay some of the instruments belonging to John Hall, a doctor and Shakespeare's son in law.

The knife glinted in a shaft of sunlight. Geoffrey had an intense desire to hold it.

On handing the children back into the care of their teacher, she pressed a £2 coin into his hand.

'I've never seen them so interested. Thank you. I've managed to have a lovely quiet cup of coffee.'

After they had left, Geoffrey went back to look at the knife, wondering what it would be like to kill someone. He turned as Esther's heels assaulted the floor behind him.

'Geoffrey. I'm so very impressed with you. You had those dear children quite under your spell.'

'As with every group I lead, surely?'

'That goes without saying.'

Geoffrey was certain Esther was up to something, so he remained non-committal and gave a gracious incline of his head.

'Thank you.'

'I think you are too modest, Geoffrey. So I've taken it upon myself to tell Jane. I thought she ought to know just how good you are.'

'So kind.'

'Don't mention it. You know I always believe in supporting my colleagues.'

Esther turned as if to walk away, then, pretending an afterthought moved back towards him.

'Oh and, you will be delighted, I've persuaded Jane to book every school group in with you from now on. Congratulations.'

With a cocky toss of her head and a deep-throated laugh, Esther flounced off, leaving Geoffrey in shock and facing a dismal future full of noisy, uninterested schoolchildren.

Wednesday was Esther's night to lock up so Geoffrey could leave early for his choir practice. Before he left, Geoffrey sought Esther's advice as to whether the minor scratch on the bedpost in the upper bedroom should be recorded in the damage book.

The knife, hard and cold, felt good in his hands. At first, he was clumsy, couldn't get enough power in his downwards strokes, until the years of frustration began to fuel his muscles.

Once she lay still, stopped resisting his blows, he paused, standing back to view his handiwork. She no longer looked bossy and self-important but dishevelled and messy, her white blouse red with blood.

Before taking off his cheap raincoat, Geoffrey pulled up Esther's skirt to display her plump legs and just an inch of plain pink knickers. She would hate that, especially in the forensic photos.

On the way home, Geoffrey disposed of the coat in a rubbish bin several streets away. The knife he had left at the scene after wiping off his finger prints. He cleaned the display items once a month so if any of his DNA remained it made an easy explanation. Moreover, as he pointed out to the police, the key to the cabinet hung in the office, the door of which was often left open and visible to the public.

At home, Geoffrey washed himself and his clothes, before heading out to his choir practice, arriving early as usual to set out the chairs.

The house remained closed for two months, causing Geoffrey to be deployed between the other Shakespeare properties, none of which suited quite as well.

Finally, the day came to return. Excited, he arrived early and began his careful preparation, dusting and polishing, fetching in flowers from the garden, before sitting with the sun on his face in the parlour, drinking in the peace before the first visitors came.

Then, the sun dimmed, as if a dense thundercloud had passed in between them. He gave a shiver, time to open the house to the visitors. Taking a last glance around to make sure everything was in order; he was shocked to find the oak table strewn with petals, leaving forlorn stalks where only minutes ago flowers had flourished.

Puzzled, Geoffrey picked up the petals and held them in the palm of his hand. They smelt the same and showed no sign of damage. Then, a deep rumble came from the old chimney. Suddenly, a massive cloud of soot burst out to cover both him and his spotless parlour.

Coughing and spluttering, he heard a low, deep laugh, almost a growl. He shivered and a creeping dread rose within him. Esther. She was here, locked in his house. The place where he had murdered her. He stood rooted to the spot.

'Tut, tut, you'd better be quick to clean this up Geoffrey. But I wouldn't bother too much, because I am going to do it again and again. I am going to make your life a misery.' Her laugh echoed between the walls and bounced off the beams.

Shards from the Bards

Geoffrey ran past his surprised visitors, past the church, neglecting his salute to Shakespeare, face and clothes blackened with soot. He didn't stop until he arrived home where he was found three days later, dead from a heart attack, the petals still clutched in his hand.

© JJ Franklin, 2014

Open Book

The Passing Bell tolled once more and, as if on cue, the clouds lifted, letting the August sunlight into the dismal chamber. Its entrance through the leaded window-panes created a dozen fragmented rainbows and set them dancing across whitewashed walls. Stiff from the morning's bedside vigil, Richard gave up all pretence of prayer and despite what had happened the last time, spoke out.

'She moved, Mother. Grandmother moved again. I swear it!'

Did I?

His mother looked up sharply and turned towards him, her clenched fingers uncurling to reveal the flat, hard palm of her hand.

'I'm warning you, boy. I've had enough of your fooling for one day.'

'But – '

He looked suspiciously at the shrunken old woman, propped up against the pillows, as still as a statue, staring silently at nothing, as she had done for the past three days.

Boo!

'I – I'm sure she did.'

His mother raised her hand but, from nowhere it seemed, Aunt Susanna appeared in front of him, shielding him from her wrath.

'No more, Judith. Please. Not today. They're only babes.'

'Babes! He's six, Susanna. They will not encourage his stories at school. 'Tis all make-believe with him, just like his... Stories? I'll tell you what they are, boy. Lies!'

'It was probably the sun,' Susanna said, hastily. 'Suddenly shining like that, it can deceive the eyes. Was that not it, Richard?'

'I – I suppose so, aunt.'

She nodded gravely and placed her arm around his shoulders.

'Your uncle says your grandmother will not move again. She's very near her time.'

Oh.

His mother shrugged. 'Well, if the great Doctor Hall says so – it must be true. There, Richard. It's proved. Attend to your prayers.' She glared at her other son kneeling on the opposite side of the bed, his hands dutifully clasped, his drooping head almost touching the mattress. 'And you, Tom! Wake up! I don't know what's got into the pair of them today. The devil, most like.' She nodded towards Bess, seated at the table under the window, poring over a large book; so large, it lay flat on the table, its pages spread open. 'You're fortunate, Susanna. A girl – and a good one at that. Girls are always more biddable.'

Susanna shook her head. 'Not always, eh, Bess? Continue reading. Let us hear what the good book teaches us.'

Bess gave a guilty start and shut the book quickly, a dark flush spreading up her neck, staining her cheeks an unnatural pink. 'I – I've lost my place, Mother.'

'Yes. I believe you have,' Susanna said, calmly.

Any further comment was diverted by young Tom, his hands still clasped, toppling forwards against the bed and letting out a gentle snore.

Ha! Goodnight, sweet Prince.

'You're wicked boys' said Judith, shaking him awake. 'Susanna, we must – '

'You're too hard on them, Judith. Could you have remained so still at their age?'

No, indeed. Fidget, fidget, fidget, all of you. But especially you, my little rabbit, running wild with that brother of yours. Hamnet and Judith. Judith and Hamnet. Like two peas in a peascod you were. My sweet darling madcaps.

'They've been praying all morning,' Susanna said. 'Perhaps we should give the Almighty's ears a

27

rest.'

And mine.

Quietly, but not stealthily enough to evade her mother's eyes, Bess pushed the book away and opened the family Bible lying next to it.

'A time to be born and a – a time to die. A time to plant and a time to – '

The bell tolled again.

'Oh, for pity's sake, how many more? It sounds so sad.'

'Eleven,' said Richard, and looked up at his protector. 'There'll be eleven more bells, aunt. I've been counting. Fifty-six have rung already. Eleven more make sixty-seven. One for each year. Grandmother is very old, isn't she? But I can count up to a hundred!'

Clever little sod.

'Indeed,' said Susanna. 'You will do well at school, Richard, but I think you should put counting aside for a time. If your aunt is willing, Bess, take the boys into the garden – but be sure they make no noise. And, Bess.'

'Yes, Mother?'

'Your grandfather's book. Much of it is not suitable for a girl your age. Your father would be most displeased. We will speak about it later.'

Pish, woman. The girl's near ripe for bedding. Show her what real men are like. Show her Fat Jack. Show her Hal and Antony. By all means, let her see Antony.

Judith closed the door behind their retreating backs. 'That's what comes of letting her learn to read. I told you how it would be. Filling her mind with nonsense.'

Don't show her Romeo. The boy's a fool!

Judith smiled, 'We can't have the good doctor displeased, can we.'

Susanna strode to the table and picked up the book.

'This is John's house, Judith. You will please me by showing some respect.'

The filmy cloud that passed over her sister's eyes whenever John's name was mentioned started to descend; but she ignored it and pointed to the book. 'Shall we try again, Jude? One last time?'

'Very well. But 'tis a waste of time. She neither sees nor hears.'

I hear you well enough, my girl. I always hear you. Screaming. Crying. Raging against the world. Peace, child, peace.

Although it was heavy, either of them could have managed the book alone, but it seemed right that today of all days, they worked together, even if the venture failed as it had so many times before. Judith's eyes were bright and sharp again, for the moment unclouded by memories. She ran her finger along the book's cover, tracing words that meant nothing to her then straying to the picture underneath. ''Tis a poor portrait of Father. Nothing like him.'

'No, indeed. But Master Condell says 'tis only a test piece. The engraver will make sure 'tis improved before the book is registered. I like it, though. Especially the mouth. He looks ready to laugh. As he always did. As you always did. Once.'

A spark, a fire, something lost long ago, flashed in Judith's eyes, then died. 'There's little cause for laughter, these days. Tell me again, Sukey. What does it say?'

Encouraged by the use of her childhood pet-name, Susanna took Judith's hand and helped her follow the words. 'It says,' she said, '"Mr William Shakespeare's comedies, histories and tragedies published according to the true original copies." And this,' she said, pointing to the word printed in large letters near the top of the page, 'is the word you seek to know.'

'Shakespeare?'

'Shakespeare.'

'And if my son had – if he had lived, his name would have been written so?'

'It is still his name, Judith. Shakespeare Quiney will always be his name. God rest his little soul.'

Amen, my gentle Susanna. Now, lass, now. It's time to end this.

Susanna took a deep breath. 'Judith, I am sorry my husband could not save your child. You have two fine sons. We sometimes forget - John did everything he could for him – as he does for everyone.'

''Twas not enough, Susanna.'

'No,' she said. 'Sometimes it isn't and it's not fair. But it was God's will that it should be his time. As it is Mother's today.'

Hey! I'm still here.

'We could not help little Shakespeare. Will you let us help your other boys? Richard is clever beyond his years.'

But Judith was looking at their father's portrait again, her fingers wandering over the high forehead, the dark, deep-set eyes, the full bottom lip, captured in that moment before he smiled. 'People say Richard is like him,' she said. 'They say he's clever but, I don't understand him. I didn't understand Father. All that nonsense. All those stories. Where did it get him?'

Susanna looked around the room, her gaze encompassing furniture, rugs, tapestries, the burning wax candles. 'He gave us a fine home, Jude.'

'He was never here.'

No. But I was.

Carefully, they sat on the bed, on either side of

the frail figure, once more placing the open book on her lap. There was nothing, not even a flicker of response.

Words, words, words. 'Tis too late for words.

They waited because there was nothing else they could do but, as always, Judith was the first to show signs of impatience.

''Tis hopeless, I tell you.'

It was probably true, but hope was all they had. Susanna looked up into her sister's tired but unclouded eyes and smiled, ruefully, 'John says we have to keep trying. Talking will do no harm and she may well be hearing us.' She bent her head close to her mother's ear. 'Mother? 'Tis us. Susanna and Judith.'

I *know who you are, girl. I'm dying, not deaf.*

'Look, Mother. We have something for you, Father's book. Master Condell says 'tis almost ready.'

There was no reaction. A great tide of weariness swept over her. Hope died; but the moment it died in her, it was rekindled in Judith. She leaned over and yelled directly in her mother's ear.

'It's going to sell for a pound!'

Strewth!

Nothing. The statue stayed still.

Judith's shoulders slumped. The tears she had

been controlling for days, threatened to fall, but she blinked them back, knowing they would be needed later.

'Your husband could be right,' she said. 'I say 'could', mind you. You'd better read something.' She jabbed at the page. 'There! Read that! What does that say?'

'"You - you are a fishmonger!"' Susanna said, horrified to find her voice quivering not with grief but something very akin to laughter.

'That can't be right.'

'"You are a fishmonger." That's what it says, Jude.'

'Why? 'Tis foolish and I won't have Richard being taught from this book. He's rude enough as it is.'

Susanna smiled. 'It's only rude in places.'

'He'll find them.'

Just like his grandfather.

'We have other books,' Susanna said, patiently. 'Bess likes the ones on natural history, but many of them are about foreign countries. Enough adventure for any boy.'

Elsinore. He took me to Elsinore once. In this very bed. And the next night we went to Rome. My world was here. Bohemia. Padua. Egypt. Illyria. Ah, yes. Illyria. We were shipwrecked on the coverlet, hid in the castle under the sheets. All night, we played in the forest and - No more words, children. I'm tired.

Susanna closed the book more sharply than she intended and placed it back on the bed. The church bell, which had become muted with familiarity, suddenly rang clear again and the laughter she was struggling to suppress, bubbled to the surface.

'A fishmonger. Oh, dear God, a fishmonger. Can't you see it, Judith? If John is right, they're probably the last words Mother will hear. "You are a fishmonger!"'

'I don't see that it's funny,' said Judith. But perhaps the laughter was infectious, or, perhaps, it was the strain of the last weeks. But, suddenly, it all became funny and together, sitting by their dying mother, they giggled like the little girls they once were.

And then they stopped.

Without a word to each other, they knelt, then recited together the words she had taught them as children.

'Our Father which art in Heaven. Hallowed be thy name.'

If it be now, 'tis not to come.

'Thy Kingdom come.'

If it be not to come, it will be now.

'Thy will be done.'

The readiness is all. Finish, dear ladies, the bright day

is done. And we are for the dark. Wait for me, Will. Wait.

Susanna took one dry, wasted hand in hers. 'She's ready, Jude.'

Judith, calm now, and accepting, took the other. Together, they placed their mother's folded hands over the book. When the last bell tolled and all had settled into silence, they rose as one and snuffed out the candles.

© Pam Pattison, 2014

Jealousy

It is not some green-eyed monster
That haunts childish nightmare.
It is a sick feeling within you
That aches more than you can bear.

It is some great imposter
Who stole happiness away,
A grey cloud above you
That stalks you every day.

A swelling up inside you
That sleep cannot remove.
Growing until its ugly head rears
No remedy to soothe.

But as with all our fears
We keep it locked from sight,
Behind our fixed expression
Pride masks internal plight.

And so a silent battle
For quarrels deep within,
For I did not know how much I cared
Till I gave you to him.

© Natalie Flood, 2014

The Tripod

Will had been showing his friend, Gary around his company and was taking a break to gaze out of his office window across the golf course. He loved how the sun sank down the second fairway.

'What's with the robot?'

Gary's question pulled Will back from his daydream; he glanced at his friend still sitting at the other side of the desk, who having surveyed the minimalistic room was now picking up a figurine standing on the desk. Will sat and took the model.

'This was made just after the War of the Worlds film came out in the 50s. It's a replica of the Martian tripod from the drawings by H.G. Wells. I found it in an antiques store one day, it reminded me of Johann and I had to have it. He helped me so much. I haven't told you about him have I?'

'No,' said Gary.

'It all started a long time ago. My son Ben, was about to start secondary school, so it must be fifteen years ago. I was still working part-time for Duncan Fosters and trying to get my own business off the ground. I had gone straight into sales from school and I knew all about office supplies – well that was all I knew about. Technology was moving forward so fast the market kept changing. I was trying the best I could to keep up to date with printers and fax machines, I read about all the latest machines and models hoping that product knowledge would inspire confidence. As with dealing with any new technology people are wary, some thought the technology was a fad, while others were holding out for the next model that would be better and cheaper. I had a couple of friends from college working with me but they weren't committed to the company, they were basically between things, waiting for a more permanent job to come up. That week we'd attempted to get the best deal on a fax machine to sell to our clients but spent most the time drinking coffee and debating the pros and cons of the five most popular models. On Friday afternoon we were stuck on two, at a complete stalemate. At five o'clock we flipped a coin and opted for the X745 and I escaped to the pub. I had a moan to Terry, the landlord, and watched the football. Johann had a casual job in the pub, helping Terry behind the bar when he was needed. He was working that night and overheard me talking to Terry about fax machines. He came over as I was grabbing my coat and told me I shouldn't buy the X745. He said the rollers on the paper feed were badly made and would go out of shape if the machine was used for too long – even as many as forty pages at a time would be risky.

'Johann had been working in the pub over the last couple of months. He hadn't spoken to any other punters before as far as I'm aware, just went straight behind the bar to work. A few people thought he was really odd, he was definitely an eccentric. My friends in the bar told me to ignore him, but I couldn't help wondering if he was right?

'The next day Molly went to her sister's...'

'She was your wife?'

'Yes, she was. Molly left and I had to keep an eye on Ben as he was grounded – again.

'He was being restless and annoying so I gave him some photocopying to do so he wasn't under my feet and actually doing something useful. It was a good opportunity to test what the guy in the pub had said; I connected two of the fax machines and had him send pages from one and print out at the other. We had a hundred leaflets to do. When he was about half way through the machine jammed and gave off a weird plasticky smell – the roller had melted and wouldn't roll anymore.

'I went back to the pub later and asked Terry when Johann was next in, explaining what he had said about the fax machine. He was surprised by my interest in his helper until I mentioned Johann's insight. Then Terry understood. He said Johann was very good with machines, they were his obsession. He was always tinkering with them – but not with anything useful like engines. He leaned over the bar and smirked, "He makes machines for hamsters. Little hamster cars and boats. It's a shame really." Terry explained that Johann's aunt had approached him as she worried about how Johann was going to survive; she talked Terry into giving him a couple of shifts there. Having given him the benefit of the doubt he discovered Johann's genius with machines, he had fixed the washing machine and various things – probably saving the pub hundreds.

'I met with Johann the next week after he finished an early shift at the pub and bought him dinner. I thanked him for his advice which I believed had saved the business. He said it was nothing and showed no real interest in the machines themselves and their purpose. The business and what I was trying to do meant nothing to him. We spent most the meal talking about his hamster contraptions. He started pulling drawings out of his coat pockets. He was rummaging for a couple of minutes for scribbles done on pub till slips. He talked of his current project – to build a hamster car that would turn if the hamster in the ball ran to the side. He was struggling because he needed special axles, but he couldn't get those parts without spending a lot of money on model cars. He ran through his pile of papers pausing at his favourite: his ultimate dream which was to make a walking machine powered by a ball – though he doubted it was even possible. I came away unsure if this man was a genius or a nutter who got lucky with the fax machine. I knew what most people in the bar would say but, I wasn't in a position to turn down opportunities. I made some phone calls to an old school friend working in a toy factory and got some obsolete components which I arranged to take over to Johann's flat.

'I followed his directions through an abandoned part of town to his flat, which was on the top floor of the house owned by his aunt's friend. On reaching the house it was obvious the flat was a converted loft that had been sectioned off to accommodate him. The rusty staircase leading to the apartment was only intended as a fire escape and was showing the effects of heavier use.

'Inside it was about the size of a large living room but he'd managed to fit in all of his living needs around his crazy workshop. Bits of track and gears and rods were littered around the boxes of axles and chains and such. Six large hamster cages holding his test subjects were stacked on the wall opposite the little window. Over these was a huge original War of the Worlds poster in a smart polished frame. In the evening light the glass over the picture gleamed like a lighthouse above the debris of the room. Hamster wheels ran around, one was on a small track but the rest were running loose; I nearly tripped on one as it scurried under the bed. I noticed half a pool cue under the bed clearly used to scoop them out again when they got under. He picked up the liveliest hamster ball and connected it to a generator on his desk. Under a rodent powered light he opened the present I had brought him and was so excited to be able to finish his car. We spent the evening making model cars and talking about my business, he happily answered my questions and gave me more advice. What he said was right again and our meetings in his hamster lab soon became a regular thing; about once a month I would go and see him. We would talk business for an hour or so then make little cars and boats and submarines often staying until after dark. It was the escape I needed from home and work, it was great to be a kid rather than worry about looking after one. It clearly made a big difference to Johann, having company and someone to work with, being able to share his world without being judged.

'As the business I was in changed and adapted he was the guy with the compass and the map. Our working relationship continued for over three years, until I was able to buy out the company I own now. I was focusing on sales again and didn't need Johann's help. I bought a bigger flat for him to live in – he had space for a workshop. I also found an outlet for his designs – working on film sets making machines. A lot of monsters and robots from sci-fi films of the eighties were powered by hamsters which is something they never tell you. That was good for a couple of years but was enough for him to live on. My accountant kept an eye on his finances and when the chance came I pushed him to invest the money in a pet supply company so he couldn't waste it. With the bulk of his money tied up he was safe to enjoy his salary developing his inventions. He stayed in that flat the rest of his life and although I never completely understood him in that time, I think he was pretty happy. He inspired a lot of children and adults with his machines – he had ambitious aims and he made them all except the walking machine which he eventually conceded was beyond him.'

Will looked at the model robot on his desk.

'This was his biggest goal for so long, if it

wasn't for Johann and his obsession with this, I would probably never have succeeded like I did. He was a misunderstood genius – in a different life he would have designed roller coasters or kids' toys or something, but instead he ended up fixing my business.'

Gary looked round the office again, taking in the stylish surroundings that attested to Will's success

'And what happened to Molly?' he said.

'As I worked more with Johann, I was investing more and more in the business financially, as well as the time. The going was good, so I had to make the money then to get ahead. She didn't understand, saying I was putting the stupid plans of a strange man above her and our son. We argued a lot, then she walked out and eventually met someone else and married. Ben's still around though, studying engineering at university, and will be graduating next summer. I dreamt of him working in business like me, but one Christmas he got a hamster car and that was that.'

© Chris Slater, 2014

Au Revoir Quebec

Dare say I'll never know
What brought about the rift.
The unfamiliar Gallic brogue?
The finger numbing cold?
Ah Mammy, you and Da
Perfect, winsome twosome
If you catch my drift.
You looked a picture
In the photograph! Hi-tcc!
Why ever flee a winter city
Babes in tow
To schlep by train
Through Nova Scotia's ice and snow.

Behind the black shadows of a frozen night
The ship sailed. 'Au revoir Papa, Quebec'.
Shedding tears in downtown Montreal?
Who knows?

One week on the water
The ocean air grows mild.
Cobh's damp dawn

Like others before
Welcomes a daughter home
Home to the dear sweet patter
Of fine Irish rain
To fields green and fragrant
Where the roan calves call
To the cows in the old farmyard cattle stall
Where eager sheepdogs greet you
Halfway up the lane.

© Rolf Heming, 2014

Dorothy at Mill Stream Cottage

We're good together, Harriet and I, and Emily, our little girl. I've had my share of difficulties with work, divorce, and my ex. People say I'm lucky, but I think it's how you deal with problems that life throws at you that matters. Or I'm just lucky. Nothing has fazed me so far though. It could be due to the kind of work I do. I am a Technical Solution Provider. Not a geek. I sell the stuff, the important bit. Efficiency is the key, and attention to detail. I get right to the heart of the problem immediately. No stress, no drama.

Mill Stream Cottage is our new home, but we've not yet moved in. Our dream house when we've done the jobs. But it's complete with an acre of paddock and a goat we inherited. I'm here every evening on my own doing a complete decorating job before we move in. It's dusk and I'm almost ready to head back home to the old house. My last job tonight is to bring the goat into the shed. Laugh if you wish, you'll not be the first. Me, a city man, will turn goatherd. Oh the joys of working at home! I can't wait. The decorating should be finished in a day or two, and new carpets fitted next week. I've dreamt of this for years. Oh to breathe country air. I've just got to get the goat in the shed.

'Oy! Come here! What the hell...!' I'll just get the special goat food in a jiff and she'll soon be inside. I walk to the food shed with a bucket.

'Frances Bacon!'

A thin, long tail just hurried out of the bag. Mice! And not just one! Goaty won't mind sharing, but I'd rather they found somewhere else to nest. When I look across the paddock, Goaty's heading over to the far corner. What a naughty girl. No! She's munching the neighbour's apple tree. We don't even know if they like sharing.

'Food! Goat! Food!'

I shout and call about half a mile across the paddock. But she is not budging. I bang on the wall to get her attention, but no, she is totally distracted. Talk about the grass greener on the other side. She's stubborn alright. That's goats for you, I suppose. Although I don't mind a challenge. But she's making no effort to acknowledge me calling. She's not going to beat me though. My mother never allowed pets at home and I'm not going to let that happen to our Emily. She will grow up with animals all round the house. Goaty is just the tip of the iceberg.

Oops! I think her horns are caught in those lower branches. I'd better check. It's not stopping her munching, though. I won't bother. Anything with horns bigger than my size 9s shouldn't need my protection. I'm not about to get tangled with an animal whose got that sort of armour on show. There are more ways to skin a cat. And I can tell you from experience that approaching any female in that predicament is suicidal.

Actually, I almost forgot. This goat is not as mild mannered as you might think. Dorothy is no lady. She is a man goat. That could be the problem. Maybe that is why Harriet has gotten along with her so well so far. Less said the better. Who would name a man Dorothy? That is it, I am not approaching a man with horns stuck in a thicket over yonder. Women! Why? Emily wanted the goat, and Harriet wanted the house. And here I am, stuck with both jobs. It has its perks though, because I get to tell farmyard tales at the office to jealous folk stuck in small city apartments.

'Oy! Goat! Come here!'

I bellow from the spot, but she is not budging. Hello? I'm sure she just looked at me sideways. I shift back behind a bush.

'Dotty! Aye Dotty! Food! Stop your nonsense!'

She looks up sharp. Ears pricked up, but legs still firmly planted, munching at next door's apple tree bark. It's eight o'clock, and I'm starving. Something catches the corner of my eye. Bloody hell, she's heading towards me. Something's worked. My mind is racing, and so is Dorothy. She's charging at me. I kick the bucket of food in a goatward direction. It flies everywhere, and I race to the house.

I call Harriet. I begin in a gentle way as if it's nothing.

'Why are you breathing like that?' she says. She starts questioning me as if we're dealing with a soft furry toy.

'What do you mean something's happened to the goat?' she says.

'Look, I'm telling you…'

'You've strangled it!'

'No, I've not. Well not quite. I don't know. I mean, I don't think so.'

'I'm not panicking, Stephen. Just tell me what's happened?'

'I'm trying, Harriet. I'm trying to tell you, but you're…'

'Is the goat dead?'

'No.'

'Is she hurt?'

'I don't know.'

'Why don't you know?'

'How do I know why I don't know?'

'Is she lying down with her eyes closed?'

'I think she was, but not now.'

'That's something. So have you fed her?'

'I can't.'

'Why?'

'She doesn't want it.'

'Oh dear! She can't eat? I knew I couldn't rely on you.'

'Look I have tried everything I could but I'm not a vet, am I?'

'Why does she need a vet? Has she got the rope round her neck?'

'Well she did, but not anymore.'

'So she almost strangled herself then.'

'Not really... Look, you'll have to come,' I say.

'I've just got Emily out of the bath, and I'm getting her ready for bed now.'

I have no idea what to say next. I'm trapped in my own garden with mice at one end, and a four legged escaped convict at the other. I have this strange feeling inside me. Angry and hungry. I skipped lunch. I'm aggrieved to spend money on goat food that's feeding a nest of mice, while the goat is eating next door's apple tree. This is too embarrassing for the office.

'So you've tried feeding her, and she won't eat.' Harriet's asking me the obvious. Why do women do that?

'Yes!'

'Will you calm down, Stephen. This isn't about you. It's about a dumb animal. So, she had the rope round her neck, but now she's hasn't.'

'Yes.'

'You've called her, and she won't respond?'

'That's right Harriet, that's right. Absolutely right. Look I'll admit I'm tearing my hair out here. You'll have to come.'

'Is she in danger?'

'She could be. I can't tell, can I!'

'I think you'd know if she was. Hold on, I'll have to dress Emily and we'll be over as soon as I can. I'll bring some fresh food.'

'Well Goaty is not interested in food.' But Harriet's already hung up.

I lean on the fence counting the minutes. Two minutes to get Emily into a coat and shoes. Another five to chop up some veg. Then she'd race over to the cottage. I know her. Twenty minutes tops. But I know it will seem like an hour.

At last! I can see her. Harriet is walking across the garden, quick but not quickly enough. I straighten myself and smile with relief. I want to kiss her. But I don't. She is on a mission.

'Where's Emily?' I ask.

'I told her to stay in the house. Where's Dorothy?'

I point across the yard.

'So what's the problem? I thought she would be lying down somewhere with the chains around her neck, dying or something.'

'Dying? She got out of the chains. Only the rope is around her neck now, but it's loose. She won't come.'

'So what's the problem?' Harriet is looking at me as if I'm from Venus and she's the one from Mars.

'Can't you see? I called and called. She won't come. I don't think she likes that shed.'

'Did you show her the food bucket?'

'Yes. She wasn't interested,' I said.

I watch Harriet strut out of the back door of the cottage to fetch the food she brought. There's no way that goat is interested in food, when she's already eaten half of next door's garden. Maybe now Harriet will see that having a goat is a bad idea. She reappears from the back door with a bucket full of chopped vegetables.

'Dorothy!' she calls.

Dorothy looks up. I think she's going to charge. I pull Harriet hard against me.

'Why you're shaking.'

My eyes are watering as I peer over the top of Harriet's head. The goat is merrily sauntering towards us.

'Good girl! Now eat up your dinner.' Harriet begins stroking the goat on the head as I loosen my arms from around her stomach.

'You're something!'

'I don't understand why you called me, Stephen.'

'You wouldn't believe this, but she just wouldn't come for me.'

'Did you even call her?'

'I did. I called her!'

'What did you call her?'

'Everything.'

'What do mean everything?'

'Everything! I called her everything.'

Harriet turned and faced me. The goat is there behind her now, eating from the bucket. Harriet's eyes turn as yellow as the goat's.

'That's the problem isn't it?

'It's a goat,' I said. 'It's just a goat.' I feel clammy. Perspiration drips from me all over.

'It's a goat with a name, Stephen. The goat's name is Dorothy. You can't have forgotten. We've had her for nearly a month, since we collected the keys to the house. You agreed.'

'Yes, but I didn't know it was a man goat with a woman's name. I didn't even know the goat had a name when I agreed to keeping it. Who named it Dorothy anyway? Was it you? If you did, that's just

...'

'She came with that name, Stephen. You'll just have to come to terms with it. We can't change her name just because... Well, she didn't sell your car, or take your kids and half your pension. She's our new pet.'

'Pet indeed!'

'Yes, Dorothy our pet goat, not Dorothy your ex-wife.'

© Marilyn Rodwell, 2014

Mary's Shop

Mary's shop wasn't a shop as you'd think of one today; it was the front room of her house. Her house was like ours, like all the others in the street, all joined to each other, except hers was the end one.

It had a tiny lobby that opened into the front room. Beyond that was the kitchen with stairs up to the two bedrooms, and beyond that, enclosed by high brick walls, was the yard containing the toilet and coalhouse. A door in the end wall of the yard led to the back alley.

The counter was on the right as you went into the shop, in line with the door frame. Boxes were stored along the wall opposite the counter, so that the only room for customers was about the same size as the lobby. Two customers were a crowd; any more had to wait outside. Mary didn't have much more room on her side of the counter either. She had stacked more boxes against the wall behind her, hiding the fireplace. The mirror above the fireplace was still there though, a forgotten reminder of what the room should have been.

Mary was a large Irishwoman who still had the lilt of Ireland in her voice even though she'd lived in our street for as long as anyone could remember. She had blue eyes and hair that frizzed around her head in a bright orange halo. I was fascinated by its colour but it never occurred to me to wonder if it was due to nature or the packets of hair dye she sold.

I loved going to Mary's shop. It smelt of the ham, bacon, cheese and block tobacco that she sliced by hand, usually with the same knife, and the sugar and butter she weighed out and packed into brown paper bags or greaseproof paper. She sold so many things, sherbet and soap, jelly and jam, toffee and tobacco that she often couldn't remember where anything was. Sometimes all the customers had to wait outside while she rummaged through the boxes.

There were two lines strung across the shop to carry more goods, one for pinafores, towels, tablecloths and dusters, the other for buckets, baskets and scrubbing brushes. Mary needed a stepladder to reach these items and had an ingenious invention to preserve her modesty while doing so. She had a length of elastic with a loop at the end attached to each side of her skirt. Before climbing the steps she would put the loop of elastic over each foot and this stopped her skirt riding up and showing her legs to the waiting customers.

Mum didn't send me to Mary's if she wanted anything in a hurry. There was always a long wait while Mary found her knife or the wrapping paper or whatever it was you wanted to buy and the wait encouraged the gossip that was the life blood of the street. Mum told me this was where she found out that the previous tenant of our house had killed himself. 'Well, I always thought there was something not right about old Albert, but to cut his throat like that – that was in your house y'know – blood all over the stairs and landing I heard. Had to paint it dark green to cover up the stains.'

And this was where I had my first taste of what went on in the adult world. As I listened to the waiting customers I learned which of Mrs Foley's brood had just been arrested. 'They had the police round there again last night. Carted Michael off this time.'

Here I found out that Mrs O'Leary was expecting another baby. 'You know the doctor told her she shouldn't have any more but the priest said she had to leave it to God. That's all very well, I said to her, but it won't be the priest or God looking after all them little ones, will it, if you peg out having another one?'

Mary's shop was a social service. Most of the

people in our streets worked, if they worked at all, for the big steel manufacturing plant on our doorstep. Mary was open when the men went to work on the first shift at six in the morning and still open at ten at night when the last shift started. She didn't seem to need sleep. I didn't need money when I went to Mary's, no one paid cash. Everything was bought 'on tick' and accounts were settled on Friday night when those who had a wage came home with the pay packet.

During the war, when food was rationed and you were only allowed so much every week, Mary would let people buy food with next week's coupons so that they didn't go short. She even had some stock that was so old she would let people have it without coupons. Once, when my mum had run out of tea coupons Mary gave her some of the old stock. Mum said it tasted so awful that it must have been in the shop since the First World War.

Mary's shop isn't there anymore - the steel works have swallowed it, our house and all the surrounding streets - and Mary herself is long gone. But she lives on still - in my memory.

© Gerry Smith, 2014

Rejection

'I only wanted to be with you.' He clutches a lock of auburn hair and gently savours its smell. 'I took this from you. You were distracted and didn't notice.' He brushes the lock over his nostrils playfully. 'Just a snip as a token of my love. *This should show you how much I care!*' The sound of a swollen river drifts up from below.

He looks down at a bundle of rags balancing on the parapet of the bridge. 'You should've gone out with me, Kate.' With a nudge, the bundle plummets toward the water.

© Steven Hawley, 2014

Circling Hat

'No, don't, not there! You can't...!'

Tim had pinched the hat ten minutes ago. He'd been prancing up and down with it, until nobody was watching anymore, then, discovering that it could be used as a Frisbee, he'd started a game of tricking and teasing his older brother. Quite soon, that became boring, too, and in order to involve other family members, he was now propelling the hat, circling like a flying saucer, direction river.

Liza, so far, hadn't been paying attention. The hat was pretty robust and been through worse. The fact that Tim was keeping himself busy without causing any danger to himself or others, was a greater benefit than you could normally expect headgear to deliver.

The sun was blaring down, on this late spring Sunday, promising a glorious summer. The shades of green along the river were singing in trees and shrubs, and still held a last touch of innocent spring purity. Only a few more days of silvery freshness, until the leaves would give in to sunlight and the city's dirty breath, matting their colours as usual, while the clock, stoically, would be ticking towards autumn.

Liza was too hot; she'd put the kids in shorts and sandals, her skirt should have been cool, but wasn't. The warmth came down from her head; perhaps she should have worn that hat after all. Liza felt the heat on her parting, as if her skull wasn't part of her body. Someone else's forehead tickled, so she pushed her hair aside, someone's sandal had a stone in it, so she shook her foot to get it out.

Three plus two, they were plodding along the path by the river. Leading and not to be overtaken, Tim, that compact human power plant. A battalion of mothers in top form couldn't keep up with his demand for, and output of, stimulation. Closely behind, but more laid-back, Tim's brother Jon, looking out for everybody, and for good opportunities for brotherly brawls.

In third position Liza, ready for emergency intervention, and preoccupied, wondering why her head felt so distant. What was going on inside appeared to be an isolated process for which it was impossible to identify any pattern or potential results. Sounds and pictures seemed to bounce off a padded wall and were redirected to a residual processor with minimal capacity, however, still capable of handling a walk.

Two steps behind Liza was Jack. She was trying in vain to shape an opinion on the fact that he wouldn't walk next to her. Here, the residual processor couldn't cope; it just recorded the child who was hanging on Jack's body. Was she hanging on his arm, his waist, his hand? Liza couldn't tell, and neither, where this awkward wave of helplessness came from, that was swashing ahead of Jack. The child on his body barely reached up to his chest; again and again he had to shorten his tall, thin figure by a third, when the daughter uttered another one of her short, plaintive sentences which nobody could understand from a normal height. The wave of helplessness grew a bit higher, and his eyes sent out diffuse complaints against the world and its inhabitants.

The daughter child was the same age as Tim, displaying a girl programme that Liza was struggling to understand. The girl refused any interaction with the boys, who had tried their best to solicit some form of acknowledgement.

On the whole, little Wendy's case didn't overly trouble Liza, as she didn't live with her dad and it seemed rather unlikely he would be bringing her along on his visits very often. But then, maybe a more emotional approach might have helped the case. What case?

And now the hat is lying in the nettles. Black

linen on a dense scrub of greyish green tussock. Group picture hatless:

Tim: bathed in sunlight, he is standing on the edge of the path, an excited smile in the corner of his eye, optimistically hoping for some interesting reaction from the other participants.

Jon: both arms stretched out, cut off by his brother's unexpected turn, stopped short in his instinctive attempt to catch what was thrown, his already dense eyebrows creating a frown. Three control programmes were competing in the nine-year-old's data centre: potential negative consequences of the event, potential requirement for him to sort things out, potential participation in his brother's expected fun.

Daughter: a hint of body tension showing. Still hanging onto the father figure; in the event of letting go, she might not have slumped immediately.

Father: frozen in the attempt to stretch his worked and tortured spine, shoulder blades bent forward in alertness, eyes creased in the expectation of a painful outcome.

The picture's focus lies halfway between these people and the middle of the nettle field. Here, colours are at their deepest and contours are at their most distinct, creating an emphasis on proportion.

Liza shouted by reflex. She couldn't say where this reflex came from, it wasn't from concerns about the hat. More like an alert from the residual processor that the decision required would exceed capacity. Warning against an imminent crash. There is data overload. A crash of the emergency supply is not a good idea right now.

A dog comes running towards them, whistling master, dragging lead, slobbering tongue and flaunting ears. Zigzagging between Tim, Jon and Liza, it decides to stop in front of the daughter, sniffing at her knees. Her facial features break apart, her mouth, growing far beyond itself, creates probably the most powerful scream she has uttered since birth.

Chain reaction: daughter screaming, father bends his knee, folding his long arms around her, however, as daughter doesn't stand still, he loses balance and has to support himself with one knee on the ground, his light coloured linen trousers in the dust, which quite clearly unbalances him even more. In order to show involvement, he shouts to Liza: 'Do something!'

Tim, all smiles upon seeing that his prayers for accelerated action have finally been heard, tries to jump on the shortly immobile dog lead. Now simultaneously: the dog, upon sensing a quick movement behind it, turns, ready to play. Jon, seeing his chance, approaches for a friendly pat, the dog changes direction again, thereby dragging its lead from under Tim's foot who, just having lifted the other foot, loses balance, too. True to what he learnt in his judo class, he turns the movement into a sporty backward roll. Just a pity that a stone is in the way of his head. That really hurts and his scream is followed by some really bad blasphemy one wouldn't expect at that age. The daughter suppresses a contented smile, as there is now no way of avoiding massive trouble in the boys' corner.

On the back of her retina, Liza watches her residual processor breaking down, sparks piercing the main unit's isolation and the robust standard processor taking on current tasks.

Is it the sun, last night's wine, or fallout from the fall of protective walls? A stinging headache punishes the sudden move to bend down and check on Tim's damaged scalp. From a small scratch between his hair, a tiny drop of blood had shown up, dark, harmless, and nearly dry. Scratch, blood and hair are sitting on an impressive bruise that already shows potential for growth.

A quick look around: 'We need to go home, that bruise wants cooling.'

In the meantime, the dog has been collected by its master, the remaining characters look at Liza, waiting for further instructions. There is just one, gently asked: 'Jack, you're the only one in trousers, could you please fetch the hat for me?'

Jack, the father, pulls his shoulder blades inwards again and lets his lips go very thin. He sounds just like the daughter when he says: 'But I don't like nettles. And my trousers are rather thin, they will sting through them.'

Frost. Frozen picture: Liza's neurons, racing with the propulsive force and the goodwill of an intercontinental rocket, penetrate the day's green and sunshine, picking up moments and stills like bizarre moths, breaking through the time barrier and entering shaded moments of the past eight months. Ouch! Headache.

On a wave of adrenaline, skirt or no skirt, Liza storms into the nettle field, snatching up the hat. Tim on one side, Jon on the other, she takes the short walk home, without explicitly inviting the other two to come along. Her headache is holding up a small screen that, for the time being, allows urgent thoughts to be deviated.

Jack and the girl remain standing on the path for a few moments longer, neither of them talking, exchanging looks, finally they follow.

Tim, already forgetting about his head, is kicking a pretty white pebble. Was it avoidable that, deflected by a wall, the stone has to hit a neighbour's car's bumper? Perhaps not, nor the fact that at this moment the neighbour comes out and pours massive abuse on Liza and the boys. With a slightly better controlled temper, that would have been avoidable. Seeing the ugly scene develop a few metres ahead, Jack bends down to check his daughter's laces.

They arrive at a closed door; he doesn't even use his keys anymore, just rings the bell like a stranger, the child hanging onto him, the wave of helplessness sloshing ahead. He drags himself into the armchair he prefers and the child crawls onto his lap.

Tim, on the sofa, is already sensing new excitement. The daughter whispers into her father's ear and his audible answer, that they had promised to stay until six, hits Liza's headache screen like a hammer blow.

'We need to have lunch. Do you want me to make some pasta?' asks Jack, now directed at Liza. Upon turning her head, the tiny screen crumbles.

'Do we need to? Honestly, no, I don't think there's anything we need to do together anymore.'

Suddenly, the intercontinental rocket in her mind has hit its target. Pictures and notes burn up in an almighty implosion leaving behind a black hole, where, previously, there had been a connection of sorts. Residual memories are sucked up and, along with the father and his daughter, disappear from the script.

'You'd better make your way home, now. Pack your things and don't leave anything behind,' she said. 'I might write and explain, but then, I might not.'

Jack is staring at the edge of the table. 'Will you take us to the station?'

'Sorry, no. There's a bus due in twenty minutes.'

Fifteen minutes later, Liza is standing by the window, caressing the soft shades of her philodendron, so much green inevitably reminding her of her lovely first car. Sun and rain with lots of green, and good friends, in a battered old car. Through the rear window, behind the back seats, you can see a black hat.

© Ingrid Stevens, 2014

A Toad, a Brick and a Wren

Smacking my head into a brick one morning last year was the painful action that finally resolved the riddle of the missing wren's nest.

The silence of the early spring mornings had been pierced by the shrill tumbling songs of a couple of wrens; their decibel levels splintering the grey light and gouging into my waking moments. It always made me smile.

It was a pretty safe assumption that it was the territorial song of the same couple that we would often see flit across our vision as we sat at the breakfast table, mugs of tea warming our hands, looking through the French windows into the garden.

'Troglodytes troglodytes', I would say showing off my limited Latin. It was a good name for the small dun-coloured blurs of wing-beats that busily probed the crevices and gaps around the pond's edge and the joints in the sculpture fountain, before nipping across the patio to inspect the dim cobwebby places behind the pot plants.

As their songs spilled across the days, and their

activity level increased, we realised that there must be a nest close by – but where? I found out one bright morning when tendrils of Virginia Creeper sent glancing shadows along the cottage walls and down the external cellar steps.

These steps are as Victorian as the rest of the cottage. They're steep and closed in by lichen coated Cotswold stone walls. Ferns – knife-like Harts Tongue and delicate Maidenhair Spleenwort push out from cracks in the lime mortar, and mingle with rounded clumps of Cushion Moss. The whole descent resembles a damp gully.

The final step has a deep crack at the corner where it meets the wall; a toad took up residence in its damp and cold safety a few years ago and lives on its equally cold diet of worms, beetles and slugs. Often, as I've left the cellar, I've seen its leathery, baggy shape receding silently into the tight, dark space. I love its presence there. I also love its Latin name: Bufo bufo; it seems so right.

The cellar door is wooden and the marks of the recent heavy rain had not only darkened the lower half of the planks as it splashed off the steps, but had also blown some paint off the jambs. Above the door, the lintel, a shallow arc of end-on red bricks, shows chips and dents where harder objects have knocked it during some manoeuvre up or down the steps.

It was at this point that another hard object (my head) knocked the arc when I stepped out of the cellar that morning. I went through the ritual of checking the crack in the step for the toad, and seeing nothing jumped onto the step and smacked the top of my head squarely onto a brick (Latin: Hardus head-dentus) in the lintel. The equal and opposite reaction was that I promptly sat back down on the step and watched the odd star on the screen of my watering eyelids explode into a supernova.

That very human reaction of having to blame something, anything other than my own misjudgement, meant that as I cursed quietly and vigorously rubbed the swelling egg on my head, I looked malevolently up at the lintel and the protruding bricks.

And then, through a blur of tears, I saw it! A fuzzy shape slowly resolved itself into a ball-like swirl of grass and moss in the shadowy corner between the lintel, the house wall and the cellar door. As soon as I saw the hole in the middle of the ball I knew this was the wren's nest, and the more I focused on it the more the pain subsided. Wiping my eyes, I gingerly stood up and looked closely at it.

And what a wonderful thing it was! A whirlpool of finely woven strands of dried grass, many times the length of the bird that carried them there, was embroidered with small pieces of moss, fragments of leaves, pale dog hairs, sheep's wool and tiny feathers, all cemented, mortar-like, by many cobwebs.

As the days passed so the lump on my head subsided, but the tumbling song continued ricocheting off the walls of the house. Then one evening, half-way down the steps, the wren hurtled from the nest and missed my nose by millimetres. Stooping below the lintel I thrilled at the sight of porcelain smooth eggs.

From that wonderful moment I declared the cellar to be out of bounds and I determined not to go down those steps until I felt sure the nest would have emptied.

But necessity meant that on three occasions over the next few weeks I had to break my self-imposed moratorium. One evening I lit my descent with a head-torch and as its beam swept past the nest, three tiny bulging eyed, fuzzy-headed beings with skinny necks and yellow gapes, strained towards the entrance before falling back into the darkness of the nest.

From the cellar a week later I watched as an adult wren, beak chock-a-bang full of wings and chitinous thoraxes, hurled out a sharp note from the top step; it was answered by cheeping from the nest. Again it happened, and again, as the physical distance between the two sounds narrowed. I moved my head in time to see the adult flit up to the nest. All sounds ceased as beaks were stuffed with insects.

The third and last time was the day the nest emptied. A golf-ball sized fledgling sat in the entrance, filling the hole. 'Hello my little one', I murmured to it. 'May your life be safe in this garden.' It blinked a jet-shiny eye and shuffled back into the darkness. No other sound came from the nest – maybe it was the last of the brood or maybe the others were used to being trodden on by their sibling.

The next day the nest was empty.

Later that year a gale's vortex bowled the fountain over, plucked the nest from its dark corner and whirled it away. Strangely enough the toad vacated its lodging beneath the step sometime during the same winter.

Since then the early mornings have been quiet. The grey light and my waking moments are poorer for the silence and the descent to the cellar is now a little less interesting.

© Tim Binder, 2014

The Tramp on the Bench

The incredibly scruffy old lady sat on the park bench, her dirty, greasy hair unkempt, her old boots flapping at the soles and her tattered skirts hanging in ragged loops over holed stockings. Her grubby hands had filthy fingernails, and her cheeks had the red mottled look of a drinker.

In front of her, by the lake, a nursemaid pushed a slightly old-fashioned pram towards the gate. An urchin with a nondescript dog on a string walked in the other direction and winked saucily as he passed the nursemaid, who tossed her head.

A tall man in soldier's uniform walked past, holding a young girl by the hand. They talked and laughed into one another's eyes, obviously very much in love. A small fair-haired child ran after a ball thrown by an older girl.

A man in his late sixties, erect and straight backed, smart in overcoat and bowler hat, walked in through the park gate and sat down on the other end of the bench. He looked at the tramp with distaste and brushed his hand over his small moustache.

A group of boys ran in through the gates and past the bench, a ginger-haired boy leading them. They raced past and then one of them tripped, swearing loudly as he landed on his knees.

'Cut!' yelled the cameraman. 'Let's take it all again from the top.' He sighed and reached for his coffee.

The nursemaid, the soldier and all the others went back to their original places and stood waiting to start the scene again. As he got up from the bench to go back to the park gates, the older man looked at the tramp, and was amazed as she winked at him.

''Ello darlin',' she said in a low voice, and smiled, showing filthy, yellowed, uneven teeth. He shuddered at her familiarity and supposed she was a regular on that bench in the park and the film company had used her as a 'colourful character.' The fee for the day's filming would stop her starving, but he wondered if it would go on drink.

They did the scene again and unfortunately the urchin let go of the string holding the dog and the dog chased off after the ball, so the dog had to be caught and the whole thing set up again. This time it all worked, but they had to wait until the director and cameraman seemed happy with the scene.

By this time the light was fading and they were told that shooting was over for the day and they could all go home. Mr Enderby, the older man, got up from the end of the bench and stretched. As the tramp stood up and went to walk off, she stood on her untied bootlace and nearly fell, but regained her balance and tottered off, carrying her torn old carpet bag with the contents spilling out of the side.

Mr Enderby had almost reached out a hand to stop her falling over, but at the last minute he stopped, thinking of the 'wildlife' which probably infested the layers of the worn and tattered garments she wore. He was still thinking of this when he reached home and went upstairs to take off his outer clothes.

He brushed his hat with more care than usual, looking carefully inside in case there was something lurking, then he laid the hat on its tissue paper nest in the box, put on the lid and put the box on top of the wardrobe.

His coat received the same care, a good brushing (paying particular attention to the collar) and a careful inspection for any stains or marks before hanging it on its wooden hanger, putting the cover over the shoulders and hanging it in the wardrobe. He so hoped he hadn't picked up anything from that dreadful woman, he had been particularly careful not to brush against her when they were leaving the park.

That evening, his washing and bathing were even more meticulous than usual and he scrubbed himself thoroughly before changing into his pyjamas, drinking his cocoa and going to bed.

He thought of her several times over the weeks which followed and wondered what had brought her to her unfortunate downfall. Whatever it was, he felt that there was no real excuse for being that disgusting and even if money were short, soap and water (even cold water) were available in most toilets for some sort of a wash. He shuddered when he thought of how close she had been to him on that park bench, but was relieved that there had been no sign of louse, flea or nit on him after their encounter.

A few months later, Mr Enderby was in his local wine shop discussing with the manager the merits of two different bottles of port. There was the 'ping' from the bell over the door, and a tall and elegant lady walked in. Her grey hair was perfectly coiffed, he noted, and she was expensively dressed in a dark suit with a ruffle of pale pink at the neckline, beautifully polished low-heeled shoes, and she carried a grey leather handbag with matching gloves. She was carefully made up, with only a hint of rouge on her pale cheeks and her lipstick exactly matching the pale pink of her blouse.

'Excuse me a moment, Mr Enderby,' said the manager and he quickly picked up a box of six bottles of wine from behind the counter and held it out to her.

'We managed to get the year you wanted. Having another dinner party at Long House?' She smiled and nodded.

'It's nice to deal with someone who knows their wines,' he went on. 'Same with Mr Enderby here and his port.' He inclined his head towards Mr Enderby and she turned to him and smiled. A slight but distinctive wave of very expensive perfume came towards him as she did so.

'Oh, yes. Mr Enderby is it?' she said. 'I think we've met before.' He was astonished, as he would have remembered her.

'I don't think...' he began, and she smiled at him again.

'Oh, I never forget a face,' she said. 'We shared a park bench together in May, in that short film set in the park.' She leaned slightly towards him. ''Ello darlin',' she said, in a low voice with a common accent.

His mouth fell open with amazement.

'You look exactly the same as you did that day,' she said. 'But me, well I love the character parts and they always manage to find me the most amazing costumes. And those teeth, well! They were so uncomfortable that I could hardly speak, so it's as well I had no lines that day. It's such fun isn't it? And of course, I can indulge my love of fine wine with the cash I make.'

Mr Enderby stood there, mouth agape. This elegant lady was the tramp? He couldn't believe it. As she took the box of wine from the manager, she turned and grinned at Mr Enderby.

'You didn't recognise me, did you?' she said and laughed at the look on his face. Then she turned at the door. 'You really shouldn't judge a book by its cover.'

© Gwen Zanzottera, 2014.

Smallman & Bigge

Henry was not a happy man. It was 1.45 am and he was sitting in his car outside a very expensive block of apartments mulling over what he was going to tell the old man. Henry was a square peg in a round hole; the round hole being the London Metropolitan Police Force and the square peg being the only son of a retired assistant commissioner in that force. Henry was not a policeman at heart; he wanted to be an artist which, according to his teacher, he was more than good at. His father would not tolerate Henry going on to art college however, but forced him into joining the police force after completing his education. Despite his ineptitude Henry rose fairly quickly in the force, mainly on the coat tails of his father's reputation and until two weeks ago he was a detective constable, aged twenty-three, in the homicide division. However, all this changed due to the lack of a quick result into the investigation of the death of the nephew of the head of a minor Arabian principality at their embassy three weeks ago, which still remained unsolved. The incumbent prince had given him hell and it was now turning into a major international incident with serious repercussions. Henry had thus been used as a scapegoat and consequently demoted to the robberies division.

There had been a spate of robberies in the same area as the embassy, hence Henry's surveillance in his own time. He was hoping for what he did not rightly know, but felt his presence in this locality would go some way to proving his keenness to produce a "result". He raised his head and looked out of the windscreen. Just then something caught his eye. It was almost as black as pitch, there being no moon visible and limited street lighting, but he stared intently at the spot where he thought he saw a movement. Sure enough he could just make out a figure, a lighter shadow within the darkness, and it was descending the building with the litheness of an acrobat at the circus. He quietly got out of his car and gently pushed the door to without engaging the lock so as not to make a noise, then crept over to the base of the building. Just as the person jumped the last five feet Henry grabbed what he thought was a young boy by the upper arm and growled, 'You're nicked son!'

He heard a soft chuckle and on turning the "boy" round he could see that he was actually holding a young woman. She was dressed from head to toe in black, so figure hugging it looked like a diver's wet suit.

'And who might you be?' she laughed. While still holding on to her arm, Henry dug into his inside pocket and produced his warrant card. Scanning it by the light of a tiny flashlight which she produced from a zippered pocket, she looked up into Henry's serious face. 'Bit of a misnomer that,' she declared, for Henry's name was Smallman and he stood 6ft 4in in his stockinged feet.

She was about to open her mouth again when he snapped, 'Don't. I've heard every single one of them.'

'I'm sure,' she replied, 'but I was about to say "snap".'

'Don't tell me your name's Smallman?' he asked suspiciously.

'Just the opposite,' she laughed, 'I'm Bigge – Samantha Bigge.'

'Yeh' he replied sarcastically.

'No really,' she declared, 'it's spelt B-I-G-G-E, and I too have been the constant brunt of cruel jokes about my height.' She stood no more than 5ft 2in in her soft flat shoes. 'Well, up to when I was 11,' she added thoughtfully.

'What happened then?' he asked, his curiosity getting the better of him.

'I broke the nose of a 14 year old boy who alluded to my size once too often,' she replied.

Despite himself Henry laughed then recovered and turned it into a cough. 'So – where are the goods?' he demanded.

Samantha smiled sweetly and batted her long, dark lashes over brilliant emerald green eyes. 'What do you mean?'

'Whatever you've stolen from up there' he replied, looking up to where she had come from. 'Come on, hand it over.'

'I don't have anything', she sighed. Henry glared at her. 'Honestly. Search me if you like.' Tempting as that prospect seemed, Henry was not fooled for a moment.

'Yeh, and if I do, you cry rape.'

They stood contemplating each other. Samantha finally broke the spell. 'What about a trade off?'

'What could you possibly offer me?' Henry asked, whilst taking in Samantha's exquisite form and wondering if he could get that lucky.

Samantha recognised the expression on Henry's face and laughed. 'No, silly, I'm talking about information.'

'About what exactly?'

'Well you remember the killing a few weeks ago in the embassy down there?'

'Don't I just,' he interrupted, 'I was on that case but got moved to robberies because I wasn't getting anywhere.'

'I happen to know who did it,' she said. He looked at her. 'No seriously.'

'How and who?'

'Well, this has to be between just you and me.'

'I'm listening,' he replied.

'Scouts' honour,' she persisted.

Henry sighed theatrically, released her arm and made the appropriate response. 'Cross my heart,' he added for good measure. He suddenly realised that he had released Samantha from his grip but she didn't try to run off, merely rubbing her arm where Henry's hand had been for the past five minutes.

She gave a small cough and smiling sweetly up at him, told how she always carried a small camera on her wrist, shoving her right hand up under Henry's nose. It was so small, not much bigger than a man's wrist watch. She didn't just relieve the rich of small baubles that they wouldn't miss but she also took photos of art work that could be useful information to certain "friends" of hers. Henry shook his head in disbelief.

'A girl's got to make a living,' she said.

'Go on,' he said.

'Anyhow, I was at the embassy that night,

outside on the balcony.'

'Weren't you frightened?' he marvelled.

'Oh, no. I've been there many times.'

'What!' he exclaimed.

Samantha made a dismissive gesture with her hand. 'All those wives in there – they've got so much disposable income they can't remember what they have. And even if they do miss something I bet they think it was one of the other wives.' Henry was amazed at her audacity. 'Well, that night I was on the balcony and I caught the whole event on my camera, through a gap in the curtains. I heard a lot of shouting so didn't move until someone said they had to make it look like a break-in and came to the window.'

Henry hadn't realised he was holding his breath until he exhaled loudly. 'What happened next?'

'I climbed off the balcony up to the roof and waited until the coast was clear before I came down at the rear.' Henry was speechless.

'So, do we have a deal?' she breathed huskily as she leaned towards him. Whilst Henry was still pondering his predicament she grabbed his tie and, pulling his head down to her level, kissed him lightly on the lips. He was so lost in the moment that he only came back to his senses when he heard a soft laugh and running footsteps.

'Meet me at the Café Gerard,' she cried over

her shoulder. 'Noon, tomorrow,' and then she was gone.

Henry touched his lips and shook his head. He got back into his car and went home to bed. The last thing on his mind was a vision of Samantha, doubting he would ever see her again and, surprisingly, a sense of loss that he had let her slip through his fingers.

The next morning, slightly heavy-eyed after his late night, he stood before his superior who demanded a progress report on the burglaries, and Henry was pleased to announce that he had a meeting with an informant later that day.

Noon found him outside the Café Gerard at a table for two. The sun was shining and it was quite warm so he had taken off his jacket, placed it on the back of the chair and loosened his tie. He was enjoying a cappuccino when the waiter came back and presented him with a large menu. He looked at his watch and noted it was 12.05 pm. Thinking he was daft to have believed her he decided not to waste the moment and, as his stomach was grumbling, having missed breakfast, he studied the menu intently. Having made his selection he put it down and there she was, sitting opposite him.

She was breathtakingly stunning in a dazzling white, sleeveless cotton dress. He was already aware of her alluring emerald eyes but the long red, wavy hair was nothing short of spectacular. He couldn't find his voice. She smiled and looked pointedly at the half drunk coffee.

'You didn't wait,' she teased.

'Um,' was all he could get out, but fortunately was saved by the waiter who appeared with a large black coffee for her.

'Your usual?' he enquired, bestowing upon her a beaming smile.

'Please, Pierre,' she replied.

'And for you, sir?' he added, his eyes still gazing adoringly at Samantha.

'Just the chicken sandwich for me.'

After the waiter had gone, Samantha sipped at her coffee then reached down into her capacious soft leather shoulder bag and pulled out a 10x8 padded envelope which she handed to Henry. He opened it and took out three black and white glossy photos. His eyebrows shot up under his hairline.

'Wow!' was all he could get out as he studied the photos of a middle-aged Arab with a curved knife in his hand which was clearly about to be thrust into the younger man.

'You know who it is, then,' stated Samantha.

'Oh yes' replied Henry, thinking of all the flack he had had to take from that particular gentleman, and his face split into a wide grin.

'You should smile more often' said Samantha, as the waiter placed a plate containing scrambled egg with smoked salmon on rye bread before her. Henry quickly put the photos back in the envelope as he took delivery of his chicken sandwich. Samantha breathed in the delicious aromas and picking up her knife and fork, cut a small corner off the bread, piled it high with egg and salmon and popped it into her mouth. She concentrated on chewing her food, digested it and breathed a sigh of pure contentment.

'Ah, that's better,' she sighed. Henry followed suit and tucked into his sandwich, neither of them saying anything until they had finished their food then she leant across the table and kissed him again before getting up and sashaying off, turning the heads of all the men in the vicinity.

Henry sat at the table with a silly grin on his face and even with the slight salty taste of smoked salmon on his lips he recognised he was definitely "hooked."

© Dianne Lee, 2014

Marie Corelli: Champion of Stratford-upon-Avon

Marie Corelli first stayed in the sleepy little country town of Stratford-upon-Avon in May 1890. She was accompanied by her great friend Bertha Vyver and Marie's half-brother Eric; they stayed at the Falcon Hotel. Nine years later, in May 1899 Marie Corelli and Bertha Vyver moved into Hall's Croft, at the time owned by a Mrs Croker. Hall's Croft is now one of the five Shakespeare Houses held by the Shakespeare Birthplace Trust.

Marie wanted to buy Hall's Croft, but Mrs Croker moved back in, so Marie and Bertha moved down the road to the Dower House.

'She needed to become part of the community, and now that she had money, she wanted to use it for the benefit of others.' (Ransom, p106)

So began Marie Corelli's series of projects for the town and its inhabitants.

1 January 1900 saw 1,000 children from Stratford-upon-Avon National Schools invited by Marie to a party at the Shakespeare Memorial Theatre, followed on 6th and 12th respectively, by

parties for 500 needy Birmingham children and 270 Stratford Infants School children. In July she paid for over 600 National School children to visit Rugby Park.

On 5 October 1900 George Boyden, the editor of Stratford-upon-Avon Herald revealed in the paper: 'outsiders would like to know that the popular novelist is still in Stratford, and that she is likely to remain here. This is an announcement that we make with a good deal of pleasure, inasmuch as Stratford cannot afford to lose one who has filled the role of Lady Bountiful so admirably.' (Ransom, pp106-07)

Unfortunately there were those in the town who did not like it when Lady Bountiful turned Lady Conservationist. Support for her began to wane due to the Faucit Memorial affair and accelerated over the draining of the Bancroft Basin.

Firstly, she learned there was a large debt on Holy Trinity church and tried to raise funds to pay it off. Sir Theodore Martin, who had already given a green marble pulpit to the church, wanted to erect a large bas-relief memorial in the chancel, opposite the Shakespeare bust, in memory of his late wife, actress Helen Faucit. He had also offered to pay the church's debt. Marie offered Rev. Arbuthnot £900 to pay off the church's debt immediately if the installation of the memorial was stopped, however he said the Bishop of Worcester had approved the memorial and it would go ahead. Undeterred, she wrote to more than 15 national newspapers, setting off a hue and cry over the desecration of Shakespeare's grave and eventually the Faucit Memorial was erected in what is now the RSC. It can be seen today at the bottom of the stairs in the Ferguson Room, Swan Theatre.

At the beginning of 1901 she took out an 18 month lease, with an option to purchase, on what had originally been an Elizabethan farmhouse called Mason Croft. In 1875, it had been bought by Dr John Day Collis, vicar, founder and headmaster of Trinity College (est.1872), next door, and Mason Croft was used for teaching. Trinity College closed in 1904, after which it was used as an army school; Marie bought it when the school left in 1908. The annexe, which was the dining hall of the College, was remodelled by Marie as her music room.

Photographs show Mason Croft with railings at the front, a portico over the entrance, Virginia Creeper on the walls, and flower-packed window boxes. After the Second World War the British Council moved in and all Marie's additions to the frontage were removed. The building is now the Shakespeare Institute, part of the University of

Birmingham.

She and Bertha took a carriage drive at the same time each day to crowds of adoring fans. If you have never heard of Marie Corelli, it is worth noting that she was the top selling author of her day. Queen Victoria was a fan and insisted that she was sent a copy of each new book. She was so famous in the United States that a city in Colorado was named after her.

The Rev. Harvey Bloom, acting master of Trinity College, introduced his daughter Ursula to Marie. Ursula Bloom went on to write over 500 novels. In 1902 the reverend and Marie fell out and she caricatured him in a 1904 novel, God's Good Man.

In 1901, she was invited to become President of Stratford-upon-Avon Choral Union and organised a sell-out concert. In July she organised a concert on the river with illuminated boats. She told the actor Halliwell Hobbes that certain factions disliked her, although she had the townspeople on her side.

In September she wrote to the Herald regarding the draining of Bancroft Basin in front of the Memorial Theatre. In the Avon Star, she called it 'one of the prettiest bits in Stratford.' However, it had been accused of smelling, but Marie said not - 'it was only the nose that was in fault. But since the unfortunate and innocent piece of water has been ruthlessly drained out and filled up, it has revenged itself by becoming a perfect distillery of objectionable odours...' (Corelli, pp140-5)

'The Council tried to ignore her, but it was the beginning of troubled times. They resented the way in which she threw her money around, though it was for good causes. Many considered that she was unnatural because she was unmarried and successfully earning her own living. Marie was fearless, outspoken, contentious and becoming a problem.' (Ransom, p111)

In April 1902 two Shetland ponies (Puck & Ariel) and an open carriage were delivered to Mason Croft; thus began a daily drive much loved by tourists.

The Henley Street Controversy started at the end of 1902, creating warring factions in the town and a bitter fight between the Town Council (commercialism) and Marie (conservationism). American philanthropist Andrew Carnegie had agreed to donate a free library to the town, and Henley Street was chosen. Four old cottages were to be demolished, along with Birch's china shop (built in 1563).

Having at first been reluctant to be involved, on 11 February 1903 Marie wrote to the Morning Post protesting against the proposed demolition of part of 'this unique old town.' (Ransom, p121) The famous actress Ellen Terry also wrote to the Morning Post in support of Marie, and Vanity Fair supported them both. Letters of support from around the world were received and printed in various newspapers. (Ransom, p122)

Marie went to see Carnegie in Scotland, but he only cared about preserving the Birthplace, and not about any other of the town's buildings. While she was there, the Town Council started to demolish the cottages.

Not trusting the local paper, Marie published Avon Star, a magazine, containing Shakespeare-related articles by various writers, plus her views on the town, the Faucit Memorial, and, of course, Henley Street.

Harvey Bloom retaliated with Errors of the Avon Star, which was an unpleasant and personal attack on Marie.

Due to the support of her by celebs of the day, including the British Archaeological Association, British Museum and Lord Warwick, the decision to establish a free library in the town became a bitter contest between the Town Council and the 'Outsiders.'

It was eventually established beyond doubt that the remaining two cottages had belonged to Shakespeare's granddaughter, wife of Thomas

Nash (see Nash's House). The library occupies what was left of the china shop; and the Birthplace Trust bookshop, the two saved cottages.

Unfortunately, there were now pro- and anti-Marie factions in the town. The bitterness culminated in her bringing an action for libel against Stratford-upon-Avon Herald, and a certain Fred Winter. There is still a Fred Winter shop in Henley Street, established in 1858, just two shops away from the library.

The anti-Marie faction published their point of view in a pamphlet in the summer of 1903, but had trouble placing it, as establishments such as Army and Navy stores and Hatchards refused to sell it.

At the subsequent libel trial, the jury found for the plaintiff but awarded her one farthing in damages. The judge observed that obviously the matter should not have been brought to trial. The farthing was eventually paid by Fred Winter, and subsequently returned by Marie via her Solicitor on 23 December 1903, 'as a contribution to one of the many Stratford charities he no doubt supports.' (Ransom, p139)

In 1903 Marie paid for the restoration of numbers 23-24 High Street, known as Tudor House. (Burley, p63)

In 1905 Marie bought a 16th century property

called Harvard House. It had belonged to the family of Katherine Harvard, whose son John founded Harvard University. It was in a rundown condition and Marie found support for its restoration amongst various rich Americans. Restoration took four years and in October 1909 it was opened by the then American Ambassador, Whitelaw Reid. Today it is in the care of the Birthplace Trust.

Also in 1909 'The Firs' was demolished. The Rev. George Arbuthnot, vicar of Holy Trinity church, lived with his wife in The Firs when Marie and Bertha first moved to the town. The garden now belongs to the town, and contains an 18th century dovecot in one corner, and a wooden notice board, that acknowledges Marie's contribution:

'This delightfully tranquil corner of Stratford was refurbished in 1990... When it was sold in 1910, Marie Corelli, the famous novelist, bought the gardens to preserve them as an open space for the benefit of the town.'

In 1913 the Guild of Stratford was established; it dealt mostly with conservation issues and Marie was on the committee. 1914 saw her chivvying the Guild to do something about the large number of trees being sold at Loxley and Welford; and the 'wanton defacement of the Waterside cottages.'

(Ransom, p192) Her secretary, Annie Davis, lived with her parents on Waterside.

1915 saw her outraged at the treatment of the avenue of trees leading to Holy Trinity church, instigated by the then vicar, Mr Melville. No doubt Marie would have something to say about the fact that, elsewhere, trees are still being chopped down.

In 1916 she was urging the Guild to pay for the uncovering and preservation of the old timbers at 30 High Street (now Currys.digital). Estimated at £75, Marie contributed £60 and the Guild £15. The premises were owned by Fred Winter.

Marie had a heart attack in January 1924, and died on 21 April. 'Stratford, on the day of her funeral, 26 April, closed its shops, drew its blinds and fell silent as their most famous resident was taken from her Mason Croft home... Hundreds of tributes poured in from high and low... The heavens wept that day and the town was a duller place thereafter.' (McFarland, no.35)

She is now largely forgotten and ignored in the town. There is only the wooden sign in The Firs Gardens, a blue plaque on the wall of Mason Croft, and a vandalised tombstone in the town cemetery.

However, despite the town's indifference, her death brought recognition of her influence in opposing modernisation in the form of a tribute printed in The Times, on 23 April 1924, from Sir Sidney Lee, Life Trustee of Shakespeare's Birthplace Trust.

'an outstanding personality, in which independence of mind, strength of will, and combativeness of spirit mingled with a genuine zeal for good causes... By her influence or at her own cost many of the houses in the town were preserved when they were threatened with rebuilding on modern lines... her intervention had the effect of modifying at a crucial point the original plan of demolition in a manner which has proved of real benefit to the Shakespeare Birthplace Trust.' (Ransom, pp205-06)

Walk around Stratford today and look at the wonderful old buildings that still exist. Thank Marie Corelli for her championship of the place. It wouldn't look the same without her.

Sources

- Bell, Maureen, *Mason Croft: A Brief History*, 2011 [Leaflet].
- Burley, Paul and Bearman, Robert *The frieze*, Stratford-upon-Avon Society, 2013 [Leaflet].
- Corelli, Marie, *An Open Letter to the Mayor and Corporation of Stratford-upon-Avon* in The Avon Star, AJ Stanley, 1903.
- Federico, Annette R, *Idol of Suburbia: Marie Corelli and Late-Victorian Literary Culture*, University Press of Virginia, 2000.
- McFarland, Patricia, *Stratford-upon-Avon in old picture postcards*, Volume 2, European Library, 1996.
- Ransom, Teresa, *The Mysterious Miss Marie Corelli: Queen of Victorian Bestsellers*, Sutton Publishing Limited, 1999.
- Stevenson, Ellie, *Stratford-upon-Avon's Other Writer: Marie Corelli*, http://www.totally4women.com/2013/06/26/stratford-upon-avons-other-writer-marie-corelli/

© Jann Tracy, 2014

Something Old, Something New

The pink fluffy feathers on the woman's hat fluttered as a soft breeze blew gently through the little chapel. It was heavily loaded with the heavenly scent of lilac and carnation, which were joyfully garlanded around the end of each pew, finished with a flourish of white and pink ribbons at their tail ends. Sunlight streamed warmly through the stained glass windows, bringing the ancient images of Mary and Jesus to life on the rich red velvet carpet.

The assembled congregation smiled in unison as Father David announced the names of the happy couple, Sarah and Ian, who stood as one at the altar, waiting to be joined in holy matrimony.

As we picked up our hymn books on cue, I let my eyes settle on the earrings I had lent to my niece, sapphire studs sparkling bright blue against the golden curls of her hair which framed her beaming face.

'Oh Aunty Kate they are beautiful and so perfect!' she had cooed when she had opened the original little brown leather casket with its gold lettering slightly worn but nevertheless still clearly depicting the high class jeweller's name.

'And they are something borrowed and something blue,' I had said, feeling rather pleased with myself, that I had made her so happy.

Sarah was my eldest sister's youngest child and unsurprisingly she looked very like me. Her wedding on 18th May was to be a very special occasion with no expense spared by her doting parents. Sarah was their only daughter.

I had worn those earrings on my wedding day, an expensive and expressive present from my fiancé.

I had met John at the local library. He had always greeted me in a friendly way and seemed genuinely interested in not only how I was but also who I was. Our exchanges grew and his visits had become more frequent. I had wondered how someone could find enough time to read quite so many books. And then it had slowly dawned on me that it wasn't the lending he was coming to the library for. We had slowly forged a friendship which we both wanted to be lasting. And so gradually, with care and nurture, it grew into something deeper, something which lived and breathed between us, which we both shared in and treasured.

'You are on the wrong page Kate,' I heard John

say, as we moved onto the last hymn. People shuffled and coughed as they prepared to sing again. The organ sprang to life and music filled the chapel to its rafters. I smiled at him, knowing that as usual he would take care of me, set me straight. But out of the corner of my eye I could still see the shaft of blue light rising up from Sarah's peachy ear lobe.

John knew that I had come with baggage and accepted that, although he was never going to be the love of my life, he could be my steadfast partner, my rock. And I could trust him beyond all doubt, which was important to me. And to my sister. She had said from the start that Sarah must never know that she was my daughter. From that moment on she had to become my niece and my goddaughter. And so I had lent my wedding earrings to my child on the occasion of her marriage. I was with her in mind and body as she made her vows and as I quietly kept those which had been made all those years ago.

© Kathy McMaster, 2014

Essential Oils

'Come on, Rob, she's wonderful.'

He was saying this to the man opposite, who sat with hunched shoulders and his chin resting on his fist. 'She has such a talent for life! I don't know how else to describe it. I know you're not keen on intellectual women, but there's so much more to her than that, believe me. I think she exaggerates the 'bluestocking with attitude' just to put some men off. It's a kind of test. I felt the same as you did when I first met her.'

His friend grunted in reply and took a drink.

'I know you're an old sceptic, Rob, so I'll never persuade you. But we've been friends a long time and you know I used to think in exactly the same way. All that laddish stuff. So, when I first clapped eyes on her, what were my thoughts? Phoar! I thought, I wouldn't mind getting inside those knickers! And my second thoughts after I'd tried chatting her up a bit was, like you said, oops, she's about as sexy as a Siberian glacier. She's got her defence system, right enough. And academic research is part of it. When she starts spouting stuff about the sexual mores of the young urban male, it's a real willie shriveller. It's like she's eyeing you as a specimen and longing to tell you what category your mating behaviour falls into. But once you get beyond that...'

'If you can be bothered to get beyond it!'

'Listen, Rob, I know you think that any woman that doesn't jump straight into bed with you is of no interest. Take it from me that some women have more to them than their bodies.'

'Unfortunately!'

'Oh, you're just being perverse. Has your current... what's her name, Pam or Pat, dumped you already? Or are you just peeved that Ellie didn't fall for your charms?'

Robin drained his glass and sat looking at his friend. His face expressed no emotion beyond a slight smile that hovered at the corner of his lips. Rather a melancholy smile thought David, as he too finished his glass and looked at his watch. Through the window of the wine bar he could see late-afternoon shoppers hurrying through the drizzle; that and the glistening twilight reminded him that he promised to be back by seven.

'Time for one more?'

'I don't have a rendezvous with a cerebral ice-maiden.'

Robin had a momentary glimpse of David's

eager, boyish face as he bent over to gather the glasses. There was also a glint of innocent triumph in his eyes but Robin ignored it. David's euphoria was unlikely to last. It never did. Throughout the years he had known him David had been through several affairs. They had all started blissfully; they had all ended in disaster and Robin had been there to pick up the pieces and encourage him to try again. Still, this latest one had caught him by surprise, and David as well it seemed.

David returned and put down the glasses. He took a thoughtful sip and said 'I think what broke the ice with me and Ellie happened by accident. But it taught me something that I should have known before if I hadn't been so naive. It was the evening after you told me you'd broken up with some woman I hadn't met. We were in this bar and you were in a foul mood; quite understandable, of course. I've been there myself and I've got a collection of misery-coloured tee shirts to prove it. But nothing I could say or do made any difference and in the end you stormed off out. At the same moment Ellie came in.

'I thought you were best left to yourself; I know those moods of yours - fierce and venomous at the time yet they blow themselves out quickly enough. Not like mine. I plunge into despair for weeks, as well you know. Anyway, in she comes and I thought she must have been meeting someone who hadn't turned up 'cause she looks around and I suppose she didn't know anyone else, but she sat down in the seat you'd just left and asked me to buy her a drink. And there was something in the way she asked that was very odd; odd for her. Well, you know how she usually sounds with that twangy, slightly nasal, rather assertive voice as though she's using it to hold you at arm's length. This time, all the oomph had gone out of her, all the in-yer-face quality that I thought was her. She looked and sounded so sad! When I brought her drink she poured it down her throat without pausing for breath. I went to get her another and by the time I got back to the table she'd perked up a bit. She sat up a bit straighter and I could see that her eyes were all red-rimmed so I said something like. 'Are you okay?' Well, obviously, I knew she wasn't but I was trying to be tactful. To tell the truth I was trying to think of ways to extricate myself. I didn't want to spend the evening with Ms Frigid Academic and I'd just seen Joyce come in. You remember Joyce; she was the dark-haired bouncy girl I met the other week? Anyway, I was aware of Joyce over the other side of the room and I was trying not to let Ellie see I was distracted by her, at the same time I was thinking, if I'm not quick Joyce is going to think I'm all tied up and go off with one of the others. So I'm composing this exit speech in my head when Ellie says, 'You're such a nice person, David.' Well, normally I wouldn't pay much attention to a stupid remark like that; I mean, coming from any other girl I've met it would have meant she wanted something from me. But coming from her, well, it didn't sound stupid. And she put her hand on my sleeve and looked sad - and sad is a stupid word to describe the emptiness in her look. And there was something about the way she said 'David'; not Dave, which would have made it sound much more casual, but David, as though she wanted to convey something important and more intimate. You know what I mean? I don't know how else to put it.'

'I get the picture.'

'It was like she was saying , 'Let's be different from the others, David.' To cut a long story short, she told me she'd been in a relationship which was going nowhere. It was no one I knew. Actually it was worse than going nowhere; it was tearing both of them to pieces. But there was another side to this torment which was the pleasure they both got out of being cruel. It was as though the cruelty they inflicted on each other sharpened them up and made the sex work. So it had become a drug. They needed it, they were addicted to it and yet they knew it was destroying them both. And a violent row brought things to a head and they ditched each other. I'm in rehab, now, she said to me with a hint of a smile. She didn't want another drink so we left and walked and I told her about my disastrous love life. It made her laugh, especially about that Russian internet date I visited in her god-forsaken town in the middle of winter. And I suddenly realised that this was the first time ever – and I mean ever – that I'd talked to a girl without any kind of hidden agenda and without any desire to pretend. I was just being myself, and I suddenly thought, this is what a real relationship must be like! It was a revelation and I tried to tell her this. I don't think I did a very good job because I'd never ever felt the need to be honest before; so I stuttered and stammered, but she understood and said that perhaps I was going into a different kind of rehab and that perhaps we could help each other through the trauma. From someone else that would have sounded corny. But it struck a real chord with me because for once in my life I wasn't trying to impress or present myself in some kind of flattering light just because I fancied her; what I fancied about her was this whole relationship thing. And I felt liberated from all the posturing and suspicion. Afterwards it seemed quite natural for her to move in with me and the absolutely amazing thing is that it still feels so natural. I mean, whenever a girl's moved in before, I've felt awkward, as though my normal life has suddenly started knocking up against corners that weren't there before. But this time, I can't believe it, it's so smooth, so hassle free; I tell you, it's quite fantastic. And we've got our routines, things we do together, things we do apart. Like, I've got my accountancy classes on a Thursday evening. I'm really fired up about them now. I'm going to get out of my dead end job and make something of myself. That's her influence, of course. And while I'm there, she's at her aromatherapy and when she comes home, it's usually a bit later than me because the girls go for a drink afterwards, but she radiates well-being. 'It's all in the essential oils,' she says. And the other week she said, 'Freedom and love are the essential oils in a relationship.' Honestly, you wouldn't call her an ice-maiden if you saw her.'

'Well, a radiant icicle! Lucky you.'

'Okay, okay. You must come round and have a meal with us one evening. Then you'd see. I know I won't convince you by talking.'

'Probably not.'

'Anyway, listen, I've got to rush. Promised I'd be back by half seven. See you next week?'

David drained his glass, turned and went,

walking briskly through the door and waving his hand without turning round. Robin sat motionless, hunched over the remains of his wine. Suddenly his mobile cheeped from the depths of his pocket. He answered it quietly.

'Yeah? Oh, it's you. We've just been having a drink or two, two minutes earlier and you'd have caught him. That might have been awkward.

What, why? No, you're so suspicious. In fact, I didn't say anything at all. He told me the story of you two meeting. *I* thought it was very touching; I hadn't heard his version before. No, no, I am being serious. Stop being so sensitive. But why should I be delighted because you're with him and not with me? And, what you mean is that he's not deliberately cruel. You know very well, that people can be cruel without knowing it, just by being utterly tedious and boring. And my god, is he tedious! And I've only had his company for an hour! But I don't want to waste my breath on him. Thank god we've got our aromatherapy to make life worthwhile. What essential oils shall I bring? Bondage flavour? Vodka as well? That sounds a great combination, I think I can manage those all right. See you tomorrow, round about six.'

© Nick Sproxton, 2014

The Broken Float

There it was again, that same under-arm cast. It was as if Grandad was avoiding an overhanging branch, but there was nothing, not so much as a twig.

And the silence...

My own float dipped. 'Feels like a perch, Grandad. A big one!'

Grandad held the mouth of the keep-net open. Then, with the hook extracted and my catch slipped into the net, he waddled back to his own peg, leaving me to select a fresh maggot: a particularly juicy maggot.

'Grandad?'

His eyes flickered and, arching his brows, he stopped chewing on his pipe, turned it over and began tapping its bowl on the flat of a stone, shedding specks of black. 'Jamie ... Jamie, d'you reckon you could see to the apples this year? On your own, I mean, without much help from me.' He raised his elbows and grimaced. 'It's a bit of a problem at the moment.'

'Yeah, of course, Grandad! You know I can.'

The basket was soon filled. The record was bound to be broken, eight boxes at least – probably more. 'Apple pie every day, Grandad!'

However, as the day wore on, the basket seemed to take longer to fill and weigh heavier with each and every lowering. Apples eluded my grasp, one in particular, touchable, but an annoying fraction too far out to give a good prod and get to swing.

After the umpteenth attempt, having witnessed me stretch and strain from every conceivable angle, Grandad lost patience and sighed. 'Come on. How many apple pies d'you think I'm going to eat? Leave that one, son. Leave it, why don't you?'

But the apple was there for the picking. Every apple would be picked, no matter how small or out of reach. One way or another, by the end of the day, the trees would be left bare – d'yer hear, God? Bare!

I stared out from the bus, brooding over my mother's words. 'You can visit Grandad on Saturday, Jamie. Just for a minute, mind.'

Rural hedgerow or suburban shop front, it made no difference. Just for a minute, mind... just for a minute – always there, played out by the rhythm and sway of the bus.

My mother leaned across me and pointed.

'That's where your Grandad worked for forty-two years.'

Huge metal shed after huge metal shed, some with a chimney belching out smoke. No windows. No trees. Just metal as black and as grey as the smoke. Factory after factory, eventually giving way to row upon row of houses, those not boarded up fitted with net curtaining and a door opening directly out onto the pavement.

My mother leaned across me again, bringing with her the nose-clogging smell of her powder. 'And that's where he was born. Number two hundred and eighty-three. I was born there, too.'

The houses ended abruptly, giving way to a wasteland backed by the skeletal forms of part-built tower blocks. There was a park; a park with a lake, its surface all speckled and splashed. As it slipped by, my mother began to gather her coat about her. She paused, tensed, ready to stand.

Grandad was in the first bed, not listening to the football commentary on the hospital radio, but lying there ... just lying there.

'Hello, Dad! My, you do look better today! Feeling better, are we? As you see, Jamie's here. Say hello to Grandad, Jamie! Been pestering to come all week, he has. Mum sends her love. Told me to tell you she'll be in tonight with Joan. Oh, and Fred from next door sends his regards. Wanted to get out on his allotment this afternoon, he did. No hope of that, though. You ought to see it, Dad! Rain? Never known anything like it, I haven't. Better off in here if you ask me. Far better.'

On and on she gabbled, bouncing her smiles off the wall, off the window, off the bed rails, directing them anywhere and everywhere other than at Grandad. Not for a moment did she even seem to notice the upturned bottles or the cylinder of oxygen and the way Grandad was fumbling with the tube inserted into his nostrils.

For pity's sake, Mum.

From behind, hands rested on my shoulders. Leave it to me, they seemed to be saying.

'Excuse me. Sorry to interrupt. It's Mrs Gorman, isn't it? Sister Mason – we've spoken before. A word, please. Before you go.'

My mother rose, straight-backed, and followed Sister, through the swing doors and away.

With the two of them gone from the ward, it left me free to edge the frame holding the cylinder of oxygen nearer the bed. Just a few inches, was all it needed. So bloody simple.

Grandad motioned with his finger, asking for water from a lidded jug stood on his locker alongside a beaker. A dry beaker, I noted, pouring

Shards from the Bards

in water and taking care not to fill it to the brim.

Grandad took a sip and held the water in his mouth: held it and held it, closed his eyes … and swallowed.

After a brief rest, he took another sip and nodded, his drinking done, the beaker to be placed back beside the lidded jug, hardly any emptier, what water had been taken appearing to have gone to the poor bloke's eyes. There would be no tears, though, not from Grandad.

The spell was broken by the sound of my mother's voice. In the few seconds left to me, before she could summon the strength to fully part the swing doors, I managed to make Grandad a promise.

Gran never cried during the service. But then, that came as no great surprise. No, the surprise came later, in the homeward-bound funeral car. It started as a rattle in her throat, then came coughing and spluttering out into the open.

Aunty Joan slipped an arm round her, placed her cheek on gran's head and gently rocked her.

Looking over at me, still rocking, my aunt softened her features, almost to the point of a smile. 'You all right, Jamie?'

'Yes, Aunty. Thank you, Aunty.'

Back at the house, there was barely room to

move. I did as I was asked and took round the sandwiches, ham in my right hand, salmon in my left. Chins wobbled, Adam's apples rose and fell, leaving me to stand and wait.

'Anyways – as I were sayin'. Flo reads instructions, like. Twenty minutes, it sez. Soak teeth fer twenty minutes. So she ponders on what she can be doin' fer twenty minutes. Dustin', her decides – oh! Ta! Don't mind if I do, lad! Anyways. Where were I? Oh ah! Dustin"

'Joan, I must say, dear. I do admire your pluck. But Blackpool? I mean – I just couldn't! Now, the Algarve, mind, where Tom and I are – Jamie! How nice! Take a sandwich, Joanny-dear. Treat yourself. Not fresh salmon, I don't suppose, poor Eth not having a deep-freeze. Which reminds me. Have I told you about my new freezer, Joanny-dear?'

'Hey! Waiter! Bringing the drinks round as well, are we? A bitter for Archie Bell, tell yer gran!'

Only the garden knew how to behave, the chrysanthemums standing to attention, the dahlias bowing their heads. They weren't telling stories about teeth or going on about holidays.

The shed door was open. Grandad never left the shed door open.

It was Uncle Tom, clearly unaware of being watched. Then, he whipped round. 'Strewth! Give a man a heart attack, why don't yer?'

The spirit-level was missing from its clips, as were the spanners. The jars of screws and the –

'Where's that little oil can of your grandfather's? Might come in handy, that. Any ideas?'

'Uncle Tom. I told Grandad I'd look after the garden. I did! I promised!'

Uncle Tom stopped squinting down the blade of a large screwdriver, placed it on the workbench, together with a pile of other tools and narrowed his eyes. 'Aaww,' he said, giving me a dismissive wave. 'There'll be more than enough for that – more than enough!'

In the garage, a man I had never met before was rummaging in Grandad's fishing basket. He looked over his shoulder at me, wrinkling his nose. 'The merry widow sent you as well, has she?'

Not waiting for a reply, he prised open a tin, picked out a fishing fly and held it to the light. 'Mm, some good stuff, here. Glad I came, now.'

Whistling, the man carried the fishing basket out to a car, rested it on the back bumper and opened the boot. In it lay Grandad's two sets of rods. The man pushed them to the back, hoisted in the basket and slammed the boot shut. Then, rubbing his hands together, he turned, then stopped, cursed and lifted up his foot. A float lay bent out of shape on the driveway. The man picked it up and held it out. 'Here. Worth waitin' for, weren't it?'

Then he patted me on the shoulder and laughed, laughing again as he entered the house. My mother, stood on the doorstep beckoning me.

'Jamie, come and say goodbye to Uncle Tom and Aunt Dorothy!'

Float in hand, I stood with my mother, dutifully acknowledging my aunt and uncle.

Uncle Tom virtually ignored me. Drumming his fingers on his steering wheel, he stared into his windscreen, forced to wait while Aunt Dorothy struggled to wedge a box of apples onto her lap.

Finally, somewhat red-faced, she beamed her farewells through the open car window. 'Bye, everybody! Bye! Keep in touch, Eth! Keep in touch now!'

I raced back to the shed. I knew what to expect, the certainty of it screaming at me. Yet, I still had to look. I just had to step inside and gaze at all the empty spaces. A shovel, the nearest thing to a spade, hung from a nail. Next to it, hung the only remaining fork, the one with a cracked and split handle. Even the mower had been taken; the practically new panther mower that was easy to push. The old one was far too heavy. Even Grandad had found it too heavy. I dragged it back a pace, gathered all my strength and pushed. It scraped along the concrete, its blades locked, bringing me to a halt.

Back home, I secured my rods to the crossbar, giving the last tie a wrench.

'I don't know how you could!' said my mother. 'Today of all days! Heaven only knows what your father would have said. Sheer disrespect, that's all it is. Sheer disrespect!'

I cast and squatted, eyes fixed on the tip of Grandad's float, at its struggle to survive, sometimes losing sight of it. Then it would reappear, turned by the current.

Something carried on the air. A familiar sound. But there was nothing. No smile. No nod. No touch on the arm. No finger pointing to where a kingfisher was about to skim the surface of the water, or to where a water rat had just entered with its customary neat 'plop'.

Nothing: just the rustle of leaves and the sound of grasses bending their heads towards the river. And, upon the breeze that bent them, the faint, yet unmistakeable whiff of pipe tobacco.

© David Nelmes, 2014

The Birth of the Bard or Having Babies in Tudor England

Four hundred and fifty years ago, a baby was born to a merchant family in a town in middle England. That child was destined to become the most famous playwright in the world but for his mother, Mary Arden, the birth would have been an ordeal, dreaded by most women. Mary was the youngest of eight children and she went on to have eight children herself, four boys and four girls. Sadly for Mary, three of her little girls died, two in infancy before William was born and one, Anne, at the age of seven years.

But what do we know of pregnancy and childbirth in Tudor England? We cannot say precisely what Mary's experience was. Textbooks for pregnant women in the mid-1500s did not exist and of course, many women weren't able to read anyway although there were books for midwives as we shall see later. The records we do have regarding pregnancy and childbirth naturally pertain mostly to the gentry since, let's face it, no-one cared about the working class sort of woman and certainly nobody wrote for them.

Pregnancy in Tudor England was a frightening experience. With medical knowledge belonging to the dark ages and most women knowing at least one person who had died in the childbed, it seems to have been approached with a form of stoical terror.

If an unmarried woman discovered she was pregnant, life could be extremely difficult. If she was a servant or working as a farm labourer, for example, the loss of income could be disastrous. Even after the baby was born it would be difficult to find work as being an unmarried mother was thought to show an untrustworthy character. Although Anne Hathaway was probably not in such dire straits as this, she might have had to make a public penance on a Sunday in front of the entire church congregation. Clearly William marrying her saved her from such a disgrace. There must have been some attempts at abortion by unmarried women but there is little direct evidence of such desperate action being taken.

Even if the woman was married and hoping to produce an heir for her husband, there was much fear associated with the process of childbirth. It was a common cause of death in women in this period and estimates give the maternal mortality rate as anything between 14-28 deaths per 1,000 women.

As there were no pregnancy kits, mistakes were often made and women were sometimes treated for illnesses they didn't have when in fact they were expecting a baby. One lady, feeling unwell and unaware of her pregnancy, instructed her doctor to bleed and purge her, the result being that she miscarried at three months.

Miscarriages were more common than today due to the poor state of health of many women. Childhood rickets caused many to have pelvic deformities and prolonged labours caused uterine muscles to become weak. In addition poor nutrition in the woman could cause her to lose her baby early on in the pregnancy.

Antenatal care did not exist in Tudor England – the middling sort of woman, like Mary Shakespeare, would probably have had access to a doctor but would have used the services of the local midwife for childbirth when the time came. At the time of Shakespeare's birth, medical science was based on humoral medicine according to the works of Hippocrates and later Galen.

Doctors believed that the human body contained a mix of the four humors: black bile (also known as melancholy), yellow or red bile, blood, and phlegm. Each individual had a particular humoral makeup, or 'constitution,' and health was defined as the proper humoral balance for that individual. An imbalance of the humors resulted in disease. The humors were also used to refer to four individual psychological temperaments: melancholic, sanguine, choleric, and phlegmatic. Therefore physical health and individual personality were inextricably linked.

There was little dietary advice given to mothers-to-be although according to humoral medicine, salads and spiced meats were to be avoided and fish and milk were too phlegmatic. Too much salt would cause the child to be born without any nails and any unusual cravings were to be ignored at all costs!

Once it was established that a woman was expecting a baby, preparations were made ahead of the birth. The woman would plan a confinement or lying-in period of about 4-6 weeks prior to the birth, depending on her status and how easily she could be spared from her duties around the house. The birth room would be prepared with the best hangings and fine decorations, the room would be kept warm and dark and sealed against fresh air as this was thought to be harmful.

Conventional wisdom of the day advised pregnant women to avoid becoming frightened or seeing ugly pictures as these were likely to harm the baby. There was even one old wives' tale that insisted the mother-to-be should not be allowed to see the full moon in case she gave birth to a mad child!

Amulets and 'magic' stones were much used to maintain a healthy pregnancy. Aetites or Eagle stone, a hollow stone with a pebble inside it, was used to prevent miscarriage and relieve the pain of childbirth. The stone was bound to the arm to prevent miscarriage but once labour had commenced, the stone was placed on the woman's abdomen or the child would supposedly not be born.

When the woman went into labour, the midwife would be called for. Midwives were licensed by the local bishop and had to swear an oath that they would baptise the child, using the correct words, if it seemed likely the child would die. Midwives were not, of course, medically trained but usually learned their craft from other midwives and also by their own experience. According to Ben Jonson, Shakespeare's friend and fellow playwright, 'Many a good thing passes through the midwife's hand, many a merry tale by her mouth, many a glad cup through her lips: she is a leader of wives, the lady of light hearts, and the queen of Gossips.' Midwives were expected to be sober, chaste and discreet.

The earliest textbook for midwives was in print

around 1540 and was a translation of a German text. Called *The Birth of Mankind* it proved extremely popular and ran to thirteen editions.

Though many midwives were unlikely to be able to read, it was common practice for a number of female friends to attend the labour 'to make good cheer' and it was frequently one of these gentlewomen who would take the book with them and read relevant passages aloud. The female friends and relatives who attended would have been invited to help and encourage the woman in labour. They would often make the mother's caudle, a drink of spiced wine or ale which would help the pregnant woman in labour to keep up her strength.

If there were complications with the labour, there was relatively little a midwife could do. Forceps were not used at the time and if the baby showed little intention of being born, an extreme solution was used, that is the use of metal hooks which not only killed the baby but slashed the mother internally. A common cause of death was puerperal fever, an infection contracted during or just after childbirth. This was the disease that killed Henry VIIIs beloved Jane Seymour.

Almond oil was often used to anoint the pregnant woman's womb and the midwife may have provided herbal infusions, poultices, and ointments to ease the process. Occasionally a birthing chair was used. This was a chair with a straight back to aid gravity with a hole cut out of the chair seat through which the midwife would deliver the newborn. Without the aid of anaesthesia, antiseptics or antibiotics, the labour was frequently an agonising and prolonged affair. Nevertheless the woman was expected to remain stoically cheerful without crying or screaming. She would ask God for a safe delivery and trust in Him.

After the birth of the baby, the umbilical cord was tied and cut and then the baby was washed and swaddled in linen bands from head to foot. Their use was intended to avoid physical deformity in the baby but frequently the bands were bound so tightly, they actually caused it to occur.

Following the birth, the mother had to remain in bed for three days. Her room was kept dark as eyesight was believed to have been weakened by labour. After three days she was allowed out of bed to sit in her chamber. This was called the 'upsitting' and was a social occasion where the mother's female friends were entertained and a meal was often served in the chamber. Following the 'upsitting' the mother was still not allowed out of her chamber for another week and the last stage of confinement was that she was further confined to the home for one more week. The end of the process was marked by the 'churching', a short ceremony where the mother would have to kneel in church while the priest read Psalm 121, the Lord's Prayer and a prayer of thanksgiving. The woman then made an offering to the church. Although it was regarded as a ceremony of thanksgiving for a safe delivery, it was popularly considered to be a ceremony of purification after the unclean process of giving birth. This practice, of course, varied, according to social status with the less well off women returning to household duties earlier than gentlewomen.

Childbirth in Tudor times, then, was no joke and sadly, without the availability of contraceptives, women had no choice at all whether they wanted to endure this terrifying ordeal. We must, however, be thankful that Mary Shakespeare did and that, on or around the twenty third of April 1564, she was delivered of a fine son. We must also be thankful that the child was not born a few months later when Stratford-upon-Avon was in the grip of the Plague – an outbreak that killed 200 of its citizens.

Bibliography

- Carson Banks, Amanda, *Birth Chairs, Midwives, and Medicine*, University of Mississippi Press: Jackson, 1999.
- Eccles, Audrey, *Obstetrics and Gynaecology in Tudor and Stuart England*, Croome Helm: London, 1982.
- Savitt, Todd L., Fevers, *Agues, and Cures: Medical Life in Old Virginia*, Virginia Historical Society, 1990.
- Sim, Alison, *The Tudor Housewife*, Sutton Publishing: Stroud, 2005.
- Aréchaga, Deborah de *Childbirth in Tudor England* http://www.agecrofthall.org/newsletter/content/view/66/27/an article by Deborah de Aréchaga

© Jennie Dobson, 2014

The Skeleton in the Cupboard

It was on the first floor, behind the books, in the cupboard marked Cleaning. The old skeleton. Her screams rang out across the building, and on my desk the paperclips rattled.

'Esme's back,' Jeremy told me, making a face, when I saw him in the common room later.

'And with a vengeance,' I added, shortly, dropping my biscuit crumbs onto the floor. Behind, I could hear our colleagues laughing. Jeremy and I weren't even smiling.

'Jackson told me it had been in the cupboard for years, he reckoned. But I still think Esme put it there.'

'That's cruel,' I said and stole a glance at my watch and exclaimed. 'I've got to go. Henry Roberts is on the warpath. See you later, as we planned?' Jeremy smiled and I brushed his hand with my own as I passed. We were in the room with a dozen colleagues. I didn't give a damn.

When I finally returned to my office, Esme was waiting, leaning against the door, smiling, her eyes like slits.

'I wondered if there was any work going? Roberts told me to come and ask you.'

'His name's Henry,' I said, mildly, thinking she acted younger than twenty. She was dressed in some kind of faded cheesecloth, a seventies throwback item, I guessed. Not that she would remember the seventies. For all her youth, I called her the witch.

'You can check these orders if you like.'

She smiled then, and I saw her eyes were an almost-brown, sparked with the brightest emerald green. Emerald Esme, I said to myself. Even her name, Esme Leverier made me nervous. Or maybe the truth was that I was jealous. She was younger than me and a great deal prettier, even in the faded cheesecloth. Jeremy was a ladies' man.

'Not with her!' he'd said to me once. 'I like my women to have a brain.' As well as the rest, is what he meant. Talk of Esme had faded and died.

Our block was in the medical wing, so all things considered, finding the skeleton wasn't that strange. It was probably once a model for teaching, now outdated and shoved at the back. But it would be Esme who found it, I thought. She made most people I knew wary. Including me.

The first time I met her, I was the new girl, making my way to a seat in the staffroom. A hand came out, attached to an arm, and pulled me back, rather abruptly. Twisting my foot as part of the deal.

'You can't sit there!' she said, sharply. 'That chair's dangerous.'

'Really?' I said. 'And how would that be?' I stared across at her lovely face.

'Women who sit in that chair get pregnant. You're not pregnant already, are you?' As she said it, she leant across and touched my stomach, ever so lightly. I flinched and stepped back, I almost thought I'd imagined her touch.

'No,' I said, 'I'm not, no,' wishing at once I'd said nothing at all. It was none of her business, if I was pregnant, or where I sat down. Surely the girl was a little deranged.

'Best not to sit in that chair then, Karen,' she said, calmly, smiling at me as she went on her way. 'Don't ever say, you haven't been warned.'

I stood there stupidly, wanting to defy her, at the same time wondering if the girl might be right. How crazy was that? I wasn't superstitious. I grabbed my tea and headed for the door, noticing then how quiet it was. All my new colleagues must have been listening. Thanks very much, I thought, bitterly. As I left I slammed the door.

When Esme had taken the orders and gone, and I was finally alone in my office, the telephone rang. Could it be Richard, coming home early? My dearly beloved absent husband was off on a jaunt at an academic conference and not coming back for a couple of days. I didn't want Richard to come home early. I needn't have worried, it was only Miss Miriman, fussing, as usual. I put down the phone and stared at my desk. As if it was a stranger, it would be soon. Me and my desk would soon be parted, and I'd be gone, and with my beloved, and not my husband. Away from the drudgery of life with Richard, my tedious job and a tedious man. And a creepy girl called Esme Leverier. A dark shadow fell across my desk.

'Esme,' I said.

'I was wondering if you had some more work?'

'No,' I told her. 'You'll have to ask Colin, I saw him upstairs.'

She nodded and smiled and turned away, but still hovered close to the doorway. *What is it now?* I thought, impatient.

'I'll see you on Monday, I guess,' she said. 'Give my love to Jeremy, won't you?'

I wondered if her words were a threat. *Damn her!* I thought, as I watched her leave. The girl was always one step ahead. I picked up my coat and my scarf from the door. I'd had enough.

Back at my house, I stared in the mirror, Esme had caused me to doubt myself. Why was Jeremy with me, really? I was far too old to be his sort of girl. I sighed and turned away from the mirror. I knew eventually Jeremy would leave me. And yet I was willing to sacrifice everything. I couldn't give up the magic of the moment.

Things never turn out the way they're meant to. A few hours later, I was sitting in the car, holding a tissue to my lip and trying to stem the blood from the split. Jeremy gripped the wheel tightly, he was driving too fast, and in the wrong lane. He also had a swollen cheek. Richard, I guessed, had a broken nose. When we'd left he'd been barely conscious. I did feel rather guilty at leaving, but staying would only have made things worse.

'So Esme was the one who told Richard?' Jeremy asked.

'So he said, and why would he say it if it wasn't true?'

'Bastard!' said Jeremy, slapping the wheel.

'Don't you mean bitch?' I said, mildly. It was late by now and I wanted to stop.

'I'll kill the cow, when I next see her,' Jeremy told me, glancing across and grinning, briefly.

'I'd rather you didn't,' I said, smiling. 'One of us has to stay in work.'

I'd only just handed my notice in and wondered if I'd gone totally crazy. Leaving my tedious husband, yes, but giving up my independence too, was that wise? *I can always change my mind*, I thought, *go in on Monday and take it all back*. But would I? I wondered.

I closed my eyes for a brief moment, and when I woke up I screamed with the shock. Right up ahead was a man in the road. A middle-aged man about Richard's age. But this was a motorway.

'Jeremy, stop!' I screamed, horrified as the car gave a lurch and some sort of shudder and moved to the right as we changed lanes fast. In just a few seconds we were back on track. But I still recalled the jar of the impact. I couldn't look back. The thoughts poured in.

That was a man, I know it was.

It doesn't really matter, we didn't hit him.

Yes we did, I felt the impact. Maybe it was Richard, it looked like Richard.

Don't be so stupid, of course it wasn't Richard.

Whoever it was, we should have stopped. Or at least looked back. I couldn't look back.

You asked him to stop, he didn't stop. It wasn't your fault.

I should have looked back.

You've already said that, now you're going crazy.

But at least being crazy's better than dead.

Don't you think?

I couldn't think, my head was on fire, it was all too much. But I couldn't deny the jar I'd felt. We must have hit that poor man. What was he doing, in the middle of the road? I felt sick.

The car drew up at our destination and we got out in silence. Later on, we talked about it. I asked him if he'd fallen asleep.

'No,' said Jeremy, 'the road was clear, and then it wasn't. That's why I had to swerve to the right.'

'But we hit him, Jeremy, we should have gone back, or stopped the car. We have to report it.'

'No we don't, we didn't hit anything. After it happened, I looked behind, in the rear view mirror and the road was empty, totally empty. I'd have noticed a man, especially if we had knocked him down. I'm not reporting something like that. They'd think I was mad.'

'Fine,' I said, and changed the subject. But why was Jeremy suddenly shaking?

'Let's go to bed,' he said to me then, and that's what we did, but it wasn't a bit like I'd thought it would be. It was wild, yes and passionate, yes, but the passion was tinged with a desperate need to block out the evening, that awful start to our beautiful life. And Esme's sneering, smug little face.

When we went back on Monday morning, we drove on the A roads, nice and quiet, except they were slower and packed with traffic. Esme was there when I got to my office.

'How was your weekend away?' she said. 'I heard you had a little disruption, everyone feeling alright, I hope?' I could have slapped her there and then.

'Go away Esme,' I said, shortly. Wishing Richard worked miles away, instead of downstairs and next to this woman. She smiled cheerily.

'He hasn't turned up for work today. That's why I'm asking.'

Richard was never seen again. When I got back to my marital home, I saw he'd packed a number of things, so at least he hadn't killed himself. Not that he would. He'd also taken the family car. He hadn't left a goodbye note, except to his boss, to say he'd resigned from his post as of then, and wouldn't be back. Which suited me fine. But I couldn't help thinking of the man we'd seen. Who'd looked just like Richard.

I suppose I should have tried harder to find him, the man on the road, I mean, not Richard. I'm ashamed to say I didn't do much. I searched the papers and looked online, searching for someone found dead on a road. I found nothing. I should have been pleased but strangely enough, I wanted an answer, perhaps I was searching for resolution. I didn't abandon my job in the end, they let me stay on, if grudgingly, because I was pregnant. I needed time off.

Jeremy had left our office by then. We only lasted another few months, the whole debacle had shaken us up. I didn't even know whose baby it was. My life was in ruins.

Except, perhaps, for my beautiful daughter.

I took Matilda to work today, for the very first time.

Everyone gathered around to see her, except for Esme, who waited until last. Her words were rather predictable.

'You shouldn't have sat in that chair,' she said.

'Go away, Esme,' I said, sourly. I was always repeating myself with her.

One of the women from Personnel, who'd most resented me staying on, came over to see me and smiled at Matilda, who was growing up fast. 'Isn't she just the loveliest thing?'

I nodded, agreeing, because, even as a mother, I knew my child was an absolute pet. Except for one thing, which nobody else but me had noticed, but it bothered me a little. My beautiful girl had the largest, enormous and earthy-brown eyes, with vibrant flecks of the brightest green. An emerald green. Then there was the way she looked at me.

Just like Esme.

© Ellie Stevenson, 2014

About the Authors

Jacci Gooding is an author and book-reviewer of independent and e-published books, based in the West Midlands. She has had several items published in traditional magazine format as well as online, and has won writing competitions. At the time of going to press, Jacci has completed her first novel and is preparing it for publication. Find her on Twitter #Jacci Gooding, or at http://www.jaccigoodingauthor.com Jacci is also a member of Bardstown Writers' and the Alliance of Independent Authors.

Sharon Hopwood is a children's writer and creator of animation concepts. A member of the SCBWI, Sharon is a popular speaker having visited many schools and literacy events, giving author talks and lively story telling sessions. Sharon is currently working on her latest series of children's books, *The Mappleford Mysteries*, which was inspired by *The Key Cutters*. Find out more at: www.hopwoodtoons.com

Bren Littlewood, writing under the pen name of JJ Franklin, has written scripts for the BBC. Her first novel, *Urge to Kill,* is a psychological thriller featuring DI Matt Turrell. The book is set in and around Stratford-upon-Avon. The second book in the series is to be published in 2014. She is a member of The Writers' Guild, The Alliance of Independent Authors and Equity. Buy *Urge to Kill* at Waterstones or on Amazon: B008K7Y47K

Pam Pattison: Pam couldn't remember a time when she didn't want to write, but publication didn't come until she was in her thirties and had some success with short stories in women's magazines. Now a pensioner, she has recently completed courses in creative writing with the Open University and was encouraged to widen her horizons and experiment with other genres including poetry and a short stage play. Currently, she is about halfway through an historical novel and admits to being easily distracted, and is toying with an idea for a children's story. So much to write – so little time.

Natalie Flood: aside from being a full time GP, and now mother, Natalie continues to try to find time for writing. She has had a couple of plays performed professionally and is currently working on a children's book, *Crassus X*, which tells the story of a pill to make you thin.

Chris Slater is a member of Bardstown Writers. *The Tripod* is his contribution.

Rolf Heming is a member of Bardstown Writers. *Au Revoir Quebec* is his contribution.

Marilyn Rodwell has had a varied career, as a teacher, nurse, business owner, and lecturer in Business. For the last few years she has been writing fiction, mainly historical fiction set between 1917 and 1930, post the Indentureship of Indian labour in the Caribbean. The first of the trilogy is *The Last Year of Childhood*, set in a small village in Trinidad, where 12 year old Latchmin is struggling to escape an arranged marriage, in order to become a teacher.

Gerry Smith's writing journey began with a creative writing course in Melbourne, Australia and she had a short story shortlisted for the Alan Marshall award there. She now has two ongoing projects. One is a collection of personal recollections of growing up in the 50s and 60s. The other is a novel, loosely based on a real murder.

Steven Hawley lives just outside Stratford-upon-Avon and spends what little free time he has putting pen to paper. He is author of *Cattle Market* (available for download on Amazon) and *Thanks For The Memory* (first prize winner of Writers' Forum magazine's national short story week competition, and later adapted for internet radio). He enjoys science fiction, fantasy and occasionally dabbles in the darker side of writing. You can follow Steven on twitter @PottyWhite.

Ingrid Stevens: word-besotted writer, blogger and translator, eternally at odds with time choices. Poems and articles published in *Pierrot*, *Die Zeit*, *Rheinische Post*, *Stratford Herald* and lots online. Her prose (young adults' journeying and science fiction) is still drawer-ridden. Find her at http://lingoservice.wordpress.com

Tim Binder: in the past Tim has written articles for various publications, and recently co-authored a book (*Walk with the Wise*) – a series of reflections on quotations from poetry and prose. Retirement has now given him the leisure and opportunity to realise a long held dream – writing a book reflecting on literature and art, as seen through his experiences of life and nature.

Gwen Zanzottera is a Cockney who has lived in the Midlands since being a child; she started writing poetry when she was seven. She has had short stories published and her verse has appeared in newspapers and anthologies and has also been performed in public. She has written murder plots for the company she performs with regularly. Gwen gives talks on various subjects, including being a Blue Badge tour guide, and has published two books on the derivation of sayings: *By Hook or By Crook*, and *One Over the Eight*, written with a fellow guide.

Dianne Lee was born in Leamington Spa and educated at the local girls' college. Just prior to retirement, she began writing children's sci-fi adventure novels and poetry. Since joining the Bardstown Writers' Group, Dianne has also written some short stories.

Jann Tracy is a recently retired proofreader. Previously, she worked in academic libraries and national museums. Jann is currently writing a number of non-fiction pieces intended for the ebook market.

Kathy McMaster has become involved with creative writing courses and writing groups over the last two years. One of her lifetime ambitions is to publish a novel. To this end she has been improving her writing skills and gaining knowledge on how to approach agents and self-publish, as well as working on her novel. She also writes short stories, mostly for competitions.

Nick Sproxton is an artist and writer who produces mainly short stories and some poetry. He is currently working on a novel for a young adult readership which explores in an imaginative way problems of identity, relationships and our fragmentary understanding of reality. These themes provide the focus for all his written work in which the fragility and insecurity of our lives is examined.

David Nelmes: a blind writer, David gave up his day job to be apprenticed to WG Stanton, a renowned BBC dramatist. This resulted in a number of short story publications, an award for his use of dialogue, an agent (now bankrupt) and the freedom to follow Dickens's advice ('once having set out my characters to play out the play, then it is their job to do it, as it were, and not mine') to guide him in the production of two novels, one first drafted and laid to grow cold, the other currently being produced in first draft.

Jennie Dobson is a freelance writer of articles, short stories and novels. At 15, she was the youngest press officer in the country, writing press releases on a daily basis. She became a freelance researcher, working with established authors and compiled an information manual for management, subsequently becoming its editor. She is currently working on an historical novel but continues to have articles published on diverse subjects. http://www.jenniedobsonwriter.com

Ellie Stevenson has written two novels, *Ship of Haunts:* (Amazon: B007SPGR98) and *Shadows of the Lost Child*, both partly historical, with a dash of the supernatural and some ghosts. *Ship of Haunts* explores life on Titanic and child migration. *Shadows of the Lost Child* looks at poverty and loss in a fictional city, and shows us what happens when time zones intersect. She has also written *Watching Charlotte Brontë Die: and other surreal stories* (Amazon: B00AZYXASU). Yet again, the work features death, destruction, ghosts and mystery (with a touch of humour). Ellie's writing is fuelled by inspiration, determination and plenty of coffee. http://elliestevenson.wordpress.com

SGPM Ltd: Simon Gooding is one of the UK's most prolific theatre production managers with a career spanning over 30 years. Starting work as a stagehand at the Bristol Hippodrome in the early 1980s, Simon soon moved on to become a production carpenter. As he toured the country he quickly accrued a technical working knowledge and appreciation of nearly all UK theatres, and in the early 1990s he ventured into production management. Since then, his experience and professionalism has ensured his name has become synonymous with large scale touring musicals, most recently *Cats, West Side Story* and *Rock of Ages*. He enjoys the challenges putting together each new show brings, and at the time of going to print he is in pre-production for the hit show *Jersey Boys*. He is delighted to sponsor this first anthology by the Bardstown Writers.
http://www.simongoodingltd.co.uk

Acknowledgements

Bardstown Writers would like to thank everyone who contributed to the production of our first anthology, particularly Ellie Stevenson, without whom this work would not exist, and proofreader Jann Tracy for her expertise. Special thanks must go to Colin Flint of Stratford-upon-Avon College and all the students who entered the cover design and logo competition. Congratulations to this year's winners, Charlie Reaper (cover) and Elliott Parkes (Bardstown Writers' logo). Last, but not least, we'd like to thank SGPM Ltd for their generous sponsorship of *Shards from the Bards*.